C

D1347484

WITHDRAWN

ESSENTIAL
IRELAND

Original text by Penny Phenix
Updated by Anto Howard

© Automobile Association Developments Limited 2009
First published 2007
Reprinted 2009. Information verified and updated

ISBN: 978-0-7495-4957-2

Published by AA Publishing, a trading name of Automobile Association Developments
Limited, whose registered office is Fanum House, Basing View, Basingstoke,
Hampshire RG21 4EA. Registered number 1878835.

Automobile Association Developments Limited retains the copyright in the original
edition © 1998 and in all subsequent editions, reprints and amendments

A CIP catalogue record for this book is available from the British Library

A03616

This product includes material based upon Crown Copyright and is
reproduced with the permission of Land and Property Services under
delegated authority from the Controller of Her Majesty's Stationery
Office. Based upon Crown Copyright and database rights LA59.
Permit number 80042

Republic of Ireland mapping based on Ordnance Survey Ireland. Permit No. 8430
© Ordnance Survey Ireland and Government of Ireland

About this book

Symbols are used to denote the following categories:

✚ map reference to maps on cover
✉ address or location
☎ telephone number
🕐 opening times
💷 admission charge
🍴 restaurant or café on premises or nearby
Ⓜ nearest underground train station

🚌 nearest bus/tram route
🚆 nearest overground train station
⛴ nearest ferry stop
✈ nearest airport
ℹ tourist information
❓ other practical information
► indicates the page where you will find a fuller description

This book is divided into five sections.

The essence of Ireland pages 6–19
Introduction; Features; Food and drink; Short break including the 10 Essentials

Planning pages 20–33
Before you go; Getting there; Getting around; Being there

Best places to see pages 34–55
The unmissable highlights of any visit to Ireland

Best things to do pages 56–77
Good places to have lunch; stunning scenery; top activities; boat trips; places to take the children; traditional music and more

Exploring pages 78–187
The best places to visit in Ireland, organized by area

Maps All map references are to the maps on the covers. For example, Cork has the reference ✚ 18L – indicating the grid square in which it can be found.

Admission prices
Inexpensive (under €5/£3.75);
Moderate (€5–€10/£3.75–£7.50);
Expensive (over €10/£7.50)

Hotel prices Room per night.
Republic of Ireland/Northern Ireland:
€/£ budget (under €100/£75);
€€/££ moderate (€100–€175/£75–£130);
€€€/£££ expensive (over €175/£130)

Restaurant prices A three-course meal per person without drinks.
Republic of Ireland/Northern Ireland:
€/£ budget (under €25/£19);
€€/££ moderate (€25–€50/£19–£37);
€€€/£££ expensive (over €50/£37)

Contents

BEST THINGS TO DO

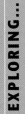

EXPLORING...

The essence of...

If your time in Ireland is limited you will need to be selective, and one of the best ways of making your selections is by asking the locals. The conversations that will inevitably ensue will be as rewarding as the information you will glean. The essence of Ireland and the friendly good humour of the Irish people are inextricably linked.

Ireland has great cities in each of its four quarters – Dublin in the east, Belfast in the north, Limerick and Galway in the west and Cork in the south – and just a short visit to each will demonstrate the differences in character between these regions.

features

Back in the 1980s, though the scenery was absolutely magical and the hospitality wonderful, there was undercurrent of sadness in Ireland at the ailing economy and the rampant depopulation, particularly among the young. Many properties were being snapped up by outsiders for use as holiday homes, which would stand empty for much of the year.

Visiting the Republic today you will find that the magic in the scenery and the genuinely welcoming people remain unchanged. But where there was concern for the future there is now great optimism. EU membership has turned the economy round, the flow of emigration has reversed and areas that were once down-at-heel are regenerated. Ireland has its own way of combining prosperity and progress with tradition and a relaxed attitude to life.

As of old, nothing is so urgent that it should stand in the way of a good conversation with someone you have only just met. Do not be deterred from visiting Northern Ireland, where the political violence has ended and you'll be impressed with the friendliness of the locals, the beautiful scenery, the interesting historic buildings and the many cultural activities.

GEOGRAPHY

- Ireland lies on the continental shelf to the west of the European mainland. To the east, over the Irish Sea, lies Britain, with Scotland 21km (13 miles) to the northeast.
- In area Ireland is 7 million hectares (17.3 million acres) and of those, around a third are devoted to agriculture.
- The largest county is Cork and the smallest is Louth.
- The highest mountain is Carrantuohill, 1,041m (3,415ft), in the Macgillicuddy's Reeks range of Co Kerry.
- The longest river is the Shannon at 340km (210 miles), while the largest lake is Lough Neagh at 396sq km (153sq miles).
- Ireland has some of Europe's emptiest and cleanest beaches, with great expanses of silvery sands and little rocky coves.
- There are thousands of lakes in Ireland, particularly in the 'lakeland counties', which extend southwards from the border with Northern Ireland, and in Connemara.
- Ireland has a large number of nature reserves that are rich in animal and plant life, and the national parks preserve some large areas of great beauty.

SPORT AND LEISURE

- Salmon season: January to September.
- Brown trout season: 15 February to 12 October.
- Sea trout fishing: June to September (or 12 October in some places).
- There is no closed season for coarse fishing, and sea angling is possible all year round.
- Ireland has over 11,000 pubs.
- There are over 400 golf courses in Ireland.

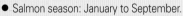

food & drink

Eating out in Ireland is as unhurried an experience as anything else in this relaxing island, and the generally high standard of cooking and service, and the quality of the ingredients, are certainly well worth savouring.

In all the major towns and cities there is a good variety of food on offer, and traditional Irish cuisine has enjoyed a revival, often with the occasional international influence. Away from the fast-food places, eating out in Ireland is not particularly cheap, but travellers on a budget will find a choice of restaurants throughout the country which offer a 'tourist menu' of good food at reasonable prices.

Specialities to look for include local cheeses, of which there are many, such as the delicious Cashel Blue, Cooleeney, St Killian, Durrus, Chetwynd Blue

and Mizen. Irish seafood is also legendary, with fresh lobster, oysters, mussels and scallops.

IRISH CUISINE

Irish cooking has a reputation for being plain but plentiful, which does it something of a disservice, because the traditional dishes have wonderfully rich flavours and interesting taste combinations.

In recent years dishes that were designed to satisfy the hunger of hard-working farmers and fishermen have been adapted to suit the lesser appetites of those who have done no more than a bit of gentle sightseeing. What was once

dismissed as 'peasant food' has now become a delicacy, such as *drisheen* (black pudding), *cruibeens* (pigs' trotters), Dublin coddle (a sausage stew), beef stewed in Guinness and, of course, Irish stew.

Potato dishes such as *champ* (mashed with chives and butter) or *colcannon* (mashed, mixed with leek, butter, cabbage, cream and nutmeg) are a tasty accompaniment, and adventurous diners can sample edible seaweed in the form of dulce or carrageen pudding.

Irish bread is not just something to make a sandwich with. There are lots of tasty varieties that only need a spreading of butter or a side dish of home-made soup. Soda bread, or wheaten bread,

made with stone-ground flour, has a wonderful flavour and texture, and there are lots of fruity tea breads such as barm brack. There is even a potato bread (mashed potato mixed with flour and egg) that is cooked on a griddle and often served with the enormous traditional Irish breakfast of bacon, eggs, sausage and black (or white) pudding.

WHISKEY AND BEER

Think of Irish beer and it is probably a pint of Guinness that springs to mind. Sold in at least 30 countries world-wide, Guinness is a great symbol of Irishness, but undoubtedly tastes best on Irish soil, with its cool, biting flavour

and thick creamy head. Hard on the heels of Guinness are two other stouts, Beamish and Murphy's, both brewed in Cork, while Smithwicks offers a smooth-tasting ale which is similar to English beer. Lager is also widely available to those who prefer a more continental taste.

Irish whiskey also has a world market and has a wonderful clean flavour, quite different from Scotch whisky or American bourbon. Four main brands are produced by the Irish Distillers company – Bushmills, Jameson, Powers and Paddy, with pure malts of various ages as well as blended whiskey. The Bushmills Distillery in Northern Ireland and the Jameson Heritage Centre at Midleton, Co Cork give guided tours which explain the distilling process.

short break

If you have only a short time to visit Ireland and would like to take home some unforgettable memories, you can do something local and capture the real flavour of the country. The following suggestions will give you a wide range of sights and experiences that won't take very long, won't cost very much and will make your visit very special.

● **Drive the Ring of Kerry** (➤ 122) to see some of Ireland's most spectacular coastal and inland scenery, including huge fiord-like bays, the country's highest mountain, sparkling lakes, pretty villages and colourful hedgerows and gardens, which flourish in an exceptionally mild climate.

● **Join in a *ceilidh*** (pronounced 'kaylee'), with traditional music and dancing. Lose your inhibitions and get lost in the atmosphere – you can always sing along. There are music sessions in the cities and large towns on most nights. In the country there is usually a session within easy reach,

especially in the west and in summer. Wherever you go the standard is generally very high.

● **Wander along Grafton Street** in Dublin, for the shops and the buskers (street musicians), and have a coffee at Bewley's Oriental Café. The variety of open-air acts is enormous, from penny-whistle players to classical string quartets. Check out the small streets off to the side; there are some good pubs to be found.

● **Go to a race meeting at The Curragh.** The Irish have a unique affinity with horses and a day at the races here is quite an experience. Visit the National Stud at Kildare (➤ 95) and see the stallions in their stalls and paddocks and learn more at the Irish Horse Museum.

● **Visit Glendalough** to soak up the atmosphere of this historic ruined monastic city (➤ 92–93) in a beautiful valley of the Wicklow Mountains. Only a short drive from Dublin, this is a world apart.

● **Look out from the Cliffs of Moher,** with no other landfall between here and North America, and contemplate the feelings of the millions of emigrants who left this beautiful country for an unknown destiny in the New World (➤ 144).

● **Visit Skibbereen on the day of the cattle market** to sample the real working life of an agricultural community, but do not be in a hurry on the road because you will be following all manner of vehicles

bringing livestock into town – all part of the experience.

● **For a taste of Ireland, eat oysters and drink Guinness** at Paddy Burke's Oyster Inn in Clarenbridge, Co Galway, famous for its oyster festival. To experience the oyster festival, visit Clarenbridge in September.

● **Rent a cruiser and explore the lovely River Shannon,** its lakes and the historic sites, riverside towns and villages along the way (➤ 64). Since the reopening of the Ballyconnell and Ballinamore Canal as the Shannon–Erne Waterway in 1994 it is possible to travel from Belleek in the north through the heart of Ireland to Limerick and the Shannon Estuary.

● **Take a walk along the clifftops of Co Antrim to the Giant's Causeway** to see how ancient travellers would first have witnessed this most remarkable place (➤ 42–43). Drive along this coast for views of cliffs, bluffs, headlands and sandy beaches.

Planning

Before you go

WHEN TO GO

JAN	FEB	MAR	APR	MAY	JUN	JUL	AUG	SEP	OCT	NOV	DEC
8°C	8°C	10°C	13°C	15°C	18°C	20°C	19°C	17°C	14°C	10°C	8°C
46°F	46°F	50°F	55°F	59°F	64°F	68°F	66°F	63°F	57°F	50°F	46°F

● High season   ○ Low season

Temperatures are the **average daily maximum** for each month. The best weather is in spring and early summer (April and June). Winter (November to March) can be dark, wet and dreary, especially in the mountainous west, but good-weather days can be magical. In high summer (July and August) the weather is changeable and often cloudy. Autumn (September and October) generally sees good weather. The cities are great places to visit at any time, regardless of the weather, and Christmas and the New Year are particularly popular.

It will almost certainly rain at some time during your stay, no matter when you visit. Be prepared, but try to accept the rain as the Irish do, as a 'wet blessing'.

WHAT YOU NEED

● Required ○ Suggested ▲ Not required

Some countries require a passport to remain valid for a minimum period (usually at least six months) beyond the date of entry – contact their consulate or embassy or your travel agent for details.

	UK	Germany	USA	Netherlands	Spain
Passport (or National Identity Card where applicable)	▲	●	●	●	●
Visa (regulations can change – check before you travel)	▲	▲	▲	▲	▲
Onward or Return Ticket	○	○	○	○	○
Health Inoculations (tetanus and polio)	▲	▲	▲	▲	▲
Health Documentation (► 23, Health Insurance)	●	●	●	●	●
Travel Insurance	○	○	○	○	○
Driving Licence (national)	●	●	●	●	●
Car Insurance Certificate	●	●	●	●	●
Car Registration Document	●	●	●	●	●

WEBSITES

Republic of Ireland

www.visitireland.com
www.discoverireland.ie
www.failteireland.ie
www.shannon-dev.ie

www.visitdublin.com
www.dublin.ie

Northern Ireland

www.discovernorthernireland.com

TOURIST OFFICES AT HOME

In the UK

Tourism Ireland (for Republic and
Northern Ireland)
103 Wigmore Street,
London W1U 1QF
☎ 0800 0397000;
www.tourismireland.com

In the USA

Tourism Ireland (for Republic and
Northern Ireland)
345 Park Avenue,
New York, NY 10154
☎ 212/418-0800;
www.discoverireland.com/us

HEALTH INSURANCE

Insurance Nationals of EU and certain other countries can get discounted
medical treatment in Ireland with a European Health Insurance Card (not
required for UK nationals), although private medical insurance is still
advised and is essential for all other visitors.

Dental services EU nationals or nationals of countries with which
Ireland has a reciprocal agreement can get discounted dental treatment
within the Irish health service with a European Health Insurance Card
(not needed for UK nationals). Others should take out private medical
insurance.

TIME DIFFERENCES

GMT	Ireland	Germany	USA (NY)	Netherlands	Spain
12 noon	12 noon	1PM	7AM	1PM	1PM

Ireland observes Greenwich Mean Time (GMT), but from late March,
when clocks are put forward one hour, until late October, summer time
(GMT+1) operates.

NATIONAL HOLIDAYS

1 Jan New Year's Day	Jun (1st Mon)	Oct (last Mon)
17 Mar St Patrick's Day	June Holiday (RI)	October Holiday (RI)
Mar/Apr Good Friday,	12 Jul Orangeman's Day	25 Dec Christmas Day
Easter Monday	(NI)	26 Dec Boxing Day/
May (1st Mon)	Aug (1st Mon)	St Stephen's Day
May Holiday	August Holiday (RI)	
May (last Mon)	Aug (last Mon)	
Spring Holiday (NI)	Late Summer Holiday (NI)	

WHAT'S ON WHEN

February *Folk Festival:* Gleneagles Hotel, Killarney, Co Kerry.

March *Dublin Film Festival.*
St Patrick's Day: various parades and pilgrimages commemorating Ireland's patron saint.

April *Irish Grand National:* Fairyhouse Racecourse, Co Meath.
World Irish Dancing Championship: the best shows, entertainments and parades at various locations.
Antiques and Collectables Fair: Dublin.

May *Fleadh Nua:* Ennis, Co Clare.
Belfast Civic Festival and Lord Mayor's Show: Belfast.
Balitmore Seafood and Wooden Boat Festival: Baltimore, Co Cork.
Slieve Bloom Walking Festival: Kinnitty, Co Offaly.
The Balmoral Show: Balmoral, Belfast.
The Cathedral Quarter Arts Festival: Belfast.

June *Limavady Jazz and Blues Festival:* Limavady, Co Londonderry.
Bloomsday (16 June): in honour of James Joyce's *Ulysses.*
Londonderry Walled City Cultural Trail: Londonderry, Co Londonderry.

July *Festival of the Erne:* Belturbet, Co Cavan.
Galway Arts Festival: films, music, books and plays.
Boyle Arts Festival: Boyle, Co Roscommon.
Historic Sham Fight: Scarva, Co Down.
Independence Day Celebrations: Ulster American Folk Park, Co Tyrone.

August *Ballyshannon International Folk Festival:* Ballyshannon, Co Donegal.

Rose of Tralee Festival: Tralee, Co Kerry.
All Ireland Music Festival: various locations.
Puck Fair: Killorglin, Co Kerry.
Killarney Arts Festival: Co Kerry.
Kinsale Regatta and Homecoming Festival: Co Cork brings expatriates home: sailing, walking and plenty of seafood.
September *Clarenbridge Oyster Festival:* Clarenbridge, Co Galway.

Galway International Oyster Festival: Co Galway.
Blackstairs Blues Festival: Enniscorthy, Co Wexford.
Story Telling Festival: Cape Clear, Co Cork.
Listowel Races: Listowel, Co Kerry.
Appalachian and Blue Grass Festival: Ulster American Folk Park, Co Tyrone.
Waterford International Festival of Light Opera: Waterford, Co Waterford.
Proms in the Park: Donegall Square, Belfast
October *Dublin Theatre Festival and Fringe Festival:* the best of Irish and international drama.
Cork Jazz Festival.
Cork Film Festival.
Kinsale Gourmet Festival: Co Cork.

Wexford Opera Festival: Wexford, Co Wexford.
Belfast Festival: at Queen's.
November *Foyle Film Festival:* Londonderry, Co Londonderry.
Listowel Food Fair: Listowel, Co Kerry.
December *Cinemagic Film Festival:* Belfast.
Dingle Wren: County Kerry. Lots of dressing up and playing tricks on 26 December.

Getting there

BY AIR

Dublin Airport

11km (7 miles) to city centre

🚆 N/A
🚌 30 minutes
🚗 20 minutes

Belfast International Airport

31km (19 miles) to city centre

🚆 60 minutes
🚌 45 minutes
🚗 45 minutes

Shannon Airport

26km (16 miles) to city centre

🚆 N/A
🚌 25 minutes
🚗 25 minutes

Scheduled flights operate from Britain, mainland Europe and North America to Dublin, Cork, Knock, Shannon and Belfast. The Republic's national airline is Aer Lingus (tel: 0818 36500; www.aerlingus.com).

Dublin Airport: By car, take the M1 south to the city centre. An Airlink bus leaves from the airport every 10 minutes, less frequently after 8pm (moderate fare, under 16s free) to the city centre via the central bus station (Busarus) and Connolly and Heuston railway stations. Taxis wait at the Arrivals area (expensive).

Belfast International Airport: The journey to central Belfast takes about 30 to 60 minutes. By car, follow the M2 motorway east. An Airbus 300 service (moderate fare, children free) runs every 10 minutes (sometimes hourly on Sundays). Taxi fares are expensive.

Shannon Airport: To get to Limerick from Shannon Airport by car, take the N18 east. Bus Éireann runs a frequent, inexpensive airport-to-Limerick/ Ennis service. Taxis are moderate to expensive.

BY SEA

Most arrivals by sea come through Dublin Port or Dun Laoghaire, south of Dublin; Rosslare, Co Wexford, has ferry links with the UK and France.

From Dun Laoghaire port by car to Dublin, simply follow signs for the city centre. There is a frequent Dublin Bus service to Dublin city centre. Taxi fares range from moderate to expensive. An inexpensive DART service (► below) from Dun Laoghaire to Dublin runs every half-hour (often more frequently).

Belfast Ferryport: the journey to Belfast takes 10 to 15 minutes, depending on traffic. Taxi fares to Belfast city centre are moderate.

Larne Ferryport: the journey to central Belfast takes 30 to 60 minutes.

Getting around

PUBLIC TRANSPORT

Internal flights Flights from Dublin to other airports in Ireland are operated by Aer Lingus (tel: 0870 876 5000), Ryanair (tel: 0871 246 0000) and Aer Arann (tel: 01-844 7700).

Trains In the Republic a limited network run by Iarnród Éireann (tel: 01-836 6222) serves major towns and cities. Trains are comfortable, generally reliable and fares reasonable. Northern Ireland Railways (tel: 028 9066 6630) operates services from Belfast to main towns and to Dublin.

A light rail overground system, the Dublin Area Rapid Transit (DART), has 30 stations from Howth and Malahide in the north to Greystones in the south (www.irishrail.ie). Trains run every 5 minutes in rush hour, otherwise every 10 to 15 minutes. Tickets are available singly from any DART station, but it is more economical to buy them *en bloc* from Dublin Bus (59 Upper O'Connell Street), from some newsstands around the city or at the stations. Tickets need to be validated by stamping them at the machine before going on the platform and boarding a train.

Long-distance buses In the Republic, Bus Éireann (tel: 01-836 6111) operates a network of express bus routes serving most of the country (some run summer only). In Northern Ireland, Ulsterbus (tel: 028 9066 6630) has links between Belfast and most villages and towns. Unlimited travel tickets are available.

Urban buses City bus services, particularly in Dublin and Belfast, are excellent. Dublin is served by Dublin Bus (tel: 01-873 4222) and the LUAS, a tram system mainly serving the Dublin surburbs (www.luas.ie). Citybus (tel: 028 9066 6630) serves the Belfast area.

Ferries Two car ferries operate between Ballyhack, Co Wexford and Passage East, Co Waterford (tel: 051-382480) and Killimer, Co Clare and Tarbert, Co Kerry (tel: 065-905 3124), the latter saving 100km (62 miles) on the road journey. There are also ferry services from the mainland to some islands.

TAXIS

Taxis are available in major towns and cities, at taxi stands or outside hotels, and at main rail stations, ports and airports. In Belfast, black cabs may be shared by customers and some operate rather like buses, shuttling their passengers between the city and the suburbs.

You can hail or stop a taxi in Dublin in the street, or you can call them by telephone (look in the *Golden Pages*). The taxis are all metered.

FARES AND CONCESSIONS

Holders of an International Student Identity Card can buy a Travelsave Stamp which entitles them to travel discounts, including a 50 per cent reduction on Bus Éireann, Iarnród Éireann and Irish Ferries (between Britain and Ireland). Contact your local student travel agency for further details. The Travelsave Stamp can be purchased from USIT, 19–21 Aston Quay, O'Connell Bridge, Dublin 2 (tel: 01-602 1906).

Many car rental companies give discounts to those over 50 or 55, as do some hotels and a few tourist attractions. Some tour companies offer special spring and autumn package deals.

DRIVING
- Drive on the left.
- Speed limits on motorways (blue): 120kph/75mph.
- Speed limits on national roads (green): 100kph/62mph.
- Speed limits on regional and local roads (white): 80kph/50mph.
- Speed limits on urban roads: 50kph/31mph (or as signposted).
- Seat belts must be worn in front seats at all times and in rear seats where fitted.
- Random breath-testing takes place. Never drink and drive.
- Lead replacement petrol (LRP) and unleaded petrol are widely available on both sides of the border. Fuel stations in villages in the Republic stay open until 8 or 9pm, and open after Mass on Sundays. In Northern Ireland, 24-hour petrol stations are fairly common. Fuel is cheaper in Northern Ireland than in the Republic.
- If you break down driving your own car and are a member of an AIT-affiliated motoring club, you can call the Automobile Association's rescue service (tel: 1800 667788 in the Republic; tel: 0800 887766 in Northern Ireland). If the car is rented, follow the instructions given in the documentation; most of the international rental firms provide a rescue service.

CAR RENTAL
All of the international car rental firms are represented. A car from a local company, however, is likely to offer cheaper rates, but may not allow different pick-up/drop-off points.

Being there

TOURIST OFFICES

REPUBLIC OF IRELAND

- Dublin Tourism,
  Suffolk Street, Dublin 2
  ☎ 01-605 7700;
  www.dublin.com
- Southeast Tourism,
  41 The Quay, Waterford
  ☎ 051-875823;
  www.southeastireland.com
- Cork-Kerry Tourism,
  Grand Parade, Cork City
  ☎ 021-425 5100;
  www.corkkerry.ie
- Shannon Development,
  Tourism Division,
  Shannon Town Centre,
  Co Clare
  ☎ 061-361555;
  www.shannon-dev.ie

- Ireland West Tourism,
  Forster Street, Galway City
  ☎ 091-537700;
  www.irelandwest.ie
- Northwest Tourism,
  Temple Street, Sligo
  ☎ 071-916 1201;
  www.irelandnorthwest.ie
- East Coast & Midlands Tourism,
  Clonard House, Dublin Road,
  Mullingar, Co Westmeath
  ☎ 044-934 8761;
  www.eastcoastmidlands
  ireland.com

NORTHERN IRELAND

- Tourist Information Centre,
  St Anne's Court, 59 North Street,
  Belfast BT1 1NB
  ☎ 028 9023 1221;
  www.discovernorthernireland.
  com

MONEY

The monetary units are (in the Republic) the euro (€), and (in Northern Ireland) the pound sterling (£). These are not interchangeable. Euro notes come in denominations of €5, €10, €20, €50, €100, €200 and €500; coins in denominations of 1, 2, 5, 10, 20 and 50 cents and €1 and €2.

Pound sterling notes for Northern Ireland are in denominations of £5, £10, £20 and £50; coins are available in denominations of £1 and £2, and 1, 2, 5, 10, 20 and 50 pence.

Provincial banks also issue notes in denominations of £5, £10, £20 and £50, but these are not accepted in other parts of the UK.

TIPS/GRATUITIES

Yes ✓	No ✕		
Restaurants/cafés (if service not included)		✓	10%
Taxis		✓	10%
Tour guides		✓	£1/€2
Porters		✓	50p/€1
Toilets		✕	

POSTAL AND INTERNET SERVICES

The main post offices in O'Connell Street, Dublin, and Castle Place, Belfast, are open extended hours, otherwise hours are 9–5:30 (Sat: 9–1/RI, 9–12:30/NI) tel: 01-705 7000 (RI); tel: 028 9032 3740 (NI).

There are plenty of internet cafés in major urban areas and the vast majority of hotels have wireless internet access of some type. Some cafés in the cities have WiFi access, usually at a small cost.

TELEPHONES

Public telephone boxes, blue and grey in the Republic and red in Northern Ireland, have been largely replaced by glass and metal booths. To make a call, lift the handset, insert the correct coins (RI: 10, 20 or 50 cents, or €1, €2; NI: 10, 20 or 50 pence, or £1) or phonecard and dial.

Emergency telephone numbers
Police, Fire, Ambulance and Coastal rescue: 999

International dialling codes
From Ireland to:
UK: 00 44
(RI only; no code needed from NI)

Germany: 00 49
USA: 00 1
Netherlands: 00 31
Spain: 00 34

EMBASSIES AND CONSULATES

UK ☎ 01-205 3700
Germany ☎ 028 7824 1300 (NI),
01-269 3011 (RI)
USA ☎ 028 9032 8239 (NI),
01-668 8777 (RI)

Netherlands ☎ 028 9077 9088
(NI), 01-269 3444 (RI)
Spain ☎ 028 9070 9348 (NI),
01-283 9900 (RI)

HEALTH ADVICE

Sun advice May and June are the sunniest months, though July and August are the hottest. Take the normal precautions against the sun.

Drugs Prescription and non-prescription drugs are available from pharmacies. In an emergency, contact the nearest hospital.

Safe water Tap water is safe to drink. Bottled water is widely available.

PERSONAL SAFETY

The national police forces are: RI – Garda Síochána (pronounced sheekawnah) in black-and-blue uniforms
NI – Police Service of Northern Ireland in dark green uniforms.

● While some sectarian tensions remain in areas like some suburbs of Belfast and southern Co Armagh, there is no longer any serious violence and visitors should have no worries.

● Take care of personal property in Dublin and avoid leaving property visible in cars.

ELECTRICITY

The power supply is: 220 volts (RI); 240 volts (NI). Sockets are three square-pin (UK type). Overseas visitors are advised to bring a good travel adaptor with them.

OPENING HOURS

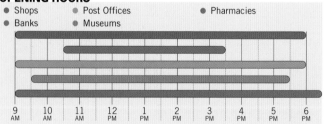

In addition to the times shown above, some shops stay open till 8 or 9pm on Thu and Fri. Smaller towns and rural areas have an early closing day on one day a week. Nearly all banks close on Saturday and many post offices close at 1pm. Museums and tourist sites vary; check with a local tourist office. Many smaller places close Oct–Mar or have very limited opening.

LANGUAGE

The Republic has two official languages, English and Irish. Everyone speaks English, though you are likely to hear Irish in the Gaeltacht areas of the west and south (Kerry, Galway, Mayo, the Aran Islands, Donegal and Ring, and Co Waterford), where you may find road signs in Irish only. Below is a list of some words that you may come across while you are in Ireland.

yes	*tá/sea*	excuse me	*gabh mo leithscéal*
no	*níl/ní hea*	how much?	*cé mhéid?*
please	*le do thoil*	open	*oscailte*
thank you	*go raibh maith agat*	closed	*dúnta*
welcome	*fáilte*	police	*gardaí*
hello	*dia dhuit*	toilet	*leithreas*
goodbye	*slán*	men	*fir*
goodnight	*oíche mhaith*	women	*mná*
hotel	*óstán*	one person	*aon duine*
bed and breakfast	*loistín oíche*	one night	*oíche amháin*
single room	*seomra singil*	chambermaid	*cailín aimsire*
double room	*seomra dúbailte*	room service	*seirbhís seomraí*
bank	*an banc*	banknote	*nóta bainc*
exchange office	*oifig malairte*	cheque	*seic*
post office	*oifig an phoist*	travellers' cheque	*seic taistil*
coin	*bonn*	credit card	*cárta creidmheasa*
restaurant	*bialann*	lunch	*lón*
café	*caife*	dinner	*dinnéar*
pub/bar	*tábhairne*	table	*tábla*
breakfast	*bricfeásta*	waiter	*freastalaí*
aeroplane	*eitleán*	station	*stáisiún*
airport	*aerfort*	boat	*bád*
train	*traein*	port	*port*
bus	*bus*	ticket	*ticéad*

Best places to see

1 Brú na Bóinne

The valley of the River Boyne east of Slane is a remarkable area containing evidence of Ireland's most ancient history.

This great neolithic cemetery consists of at least 40 burial sites, and the landscape is dotted with standing stones and earthworks, but the crowning glory is the great passage grave at **Newgrange.** Older than Stonehenge, it is a mound of enormous dimensions, 11m (36ft) high and 90m (295ft) across, with a white quartzite retaining wall encircled with large kerbstones (curbstones) at its base, incised with geometric patterns. Beyond this are the 12 surviving stones of a great circle that once stretched all the way around the mound.

The entrance to the tomb is marked by a massive stone with triple spiral ornamentations, and above it is an opening through which the rays of the rising sun illuminate the interior of the central chamber for about 15 minutes on just one day of the year – the winter solstice, 21 December (the phenomenon is re-created with artificial light the rest of the year, at the end of the guided tour).

Inside the chamber it is possible to see the intricate construction of the roof, which still keeps

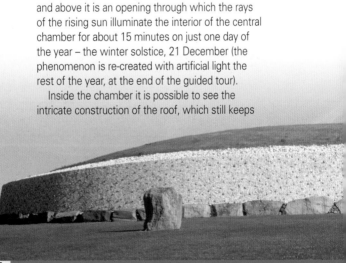

out water after about 5,000 years, and the recesses into which the remains of the cremated dead were placed, together with final offerings. There are more of the mysterious geometric patterns on the stones. Much about Newgrange remains a mystery, but there is an interpretative centre at the site which explains what has been discovered.

Try to visit Newgrange outside the peak summer season, when it can get uncomfortably crowded, with lengthy queues for the guided tour, and around the winter solstice, when it is almost impossible to get in. People book years in advance to witness the illumination of the chamber on that morning.

The other major sites of Brú na Bóinne are the two burial chambers at **Knowth,** northwest of Slane, and the larger site at Dowth, which now can only be viewed from the road.

Newgrange and Knowth

✚ 9F ✉ Donore ☎ 041-988 0300; www.heritage ireland.ie 🕐 Mar–Apr, Oct daily 9:30–5:30; May, late Sep daily 9–6:30; Jun to mid-Sep daily 9–7; Nov–Feb daily 9:30–5. Closed 23–27 Dec. Knowth: early Apr–Oct ✋ Varies according to site; visitor centre expensive 🍴 Coffee shop (€)

2 Clonmacnoise

One of the most atmospheric places in Ireland, this ancient monastic city stands in peaceful seclusion beside the River Shannon.

In AD545 St Ciaran (or Kieran) founded a monastery in this isolated place, cut off from the rest of Ireland by the wide River Shannon and surrounding bogland, and accessible only by boat. In this remote location his monastery grew into an ecclesiastical city, the most important religious foundation of its time in Ireland, and as his burial site it became a place of pilgrimage.

Over the ensuing centuries more and more buildings were added, and the ruins we see today are the most extensive of their kind in the country, including a cathedral, eight churches which were built between the 10th and 13th centuries, two round towers, three high crosses, over 600 early Christian grave slabs, two holy wells and a 13th-century castle.

A short distance away is the beautiful Romanesque 'Nun's Church', which was built by Devorgilla, wife of chieftain Tiernan O'Rourke. It was her abduction by Dermot MacMurrough, King of Leinster, that led to the conflict which resulted in the Anglo-Norman invasion of Ireland.

Clonmacnoise was also the burial place of the Kings of Connaught and of Tara, including the last High King of Ireland, Rory O'Conor, who was laid to rest here in 1198. In spite of the remoteness of its setting, Clonmacnoise was known throughout Europe as a centre of excellence in art and literature. Masterpieces of Irish craftsmanship and intricate decoration produced here include the gold and silver Crozier of Clonmacnoise and the Cross of Cong, now in the Treasury of the National Museum in Dublin (➤ 48–49), and the earliest known manuscript in the vernacular Irish, the *Book of the Dun Cow*, was produced here.

✚ 19G ✉ Shannonbridge ☎ 090-967 4195; www.heritageireland.ie ◷ Mid-Mar to mid-May, mid-Sep to Oct daily 10–6; mid-May to mid-Sep daily 9–7; Nov to mid-Mar daily 10:30–5:30 ♿ Moderate ⊪ Coffee shop end Mar–Oct (€)

3 Corca Dhuibhne (The Dingle Peninsula)

Of all the glories of the west coast, the Dingle Peninsula is the most beautiful and the most dramatic.

The Dingle Peninsula has many attractions, but best of all is its wonderful coastal scenery, which can be appreciated from the Dingle Way long-distance footpath (49km/31 miles). Along the north coast are great sweeping bays, backed by huge brooding mountains. The south has pretty little coves and the lovely Inch

beach, and in the west is the incomparable sight of the Blasket Islands off Slea Head. After exploring the coast, the drive across the Connor Pass north from Dingle and over Brandon Mountain opens up a whole new perspective, with magnificent views down towards Brandon Bay.

Dingle (An Daingean) is the main centre, a delightful town of brightly painted houses and shops with a picturesque harbour which still supports a working fishing fleet as well as pleasure craft. These include boat trips to see the famous friendly dolphin, Fungi, who lives near the harbour mouth. Dingle is a lively place with an annual cultural festival and regatta.

Ancient sites on The Dingle include a cliff-top Iron-Age fort near Ventry, Minard Castle, above Dingle Bay, and Gallarus Oratory, a tiny church dating from around the 8th century, between

Ballyferriter and Ballynana. Nearby Kilmalkedar
Church, dating from the 12th century, contains the
Alphabet Stone, inscribed with both Roman and
ancient Irish characters.

✚ 14K 🚢 Dingle Marine Eco Tours, The Pier, Dingle
(☎ 086-285 8802) operate sea tours around Dingle
Peninsula, including Blasket Islands (Apr–Oct)
ℹ️ Dingle Tourist Office, The Quay ☎ 066-915 1188

4 The Giant's Causeway

www.ntni.org.uk

This unique geological phenomenon, set on a coastline of outstanding beauty, is one of the wonders of the natural world.

About 40,000 columns of basalt cluster on the shoreline here, forming stepping stones from the cliffs down to the water. Most of them are hexagonal, but some have four, five, seven or eight sides, and the tallest rise to around 12m (39ft). The only other place in the world where such columns can be seen is on Staffa, an island off the coast of Scotland, and this is because they are part of the same formation. Little wonder that the Causeway has been designated a World Heritage Site.

The columns are the result of volcanic action some 60 million years ago, which caused molten basalt to seep up through the chalky bedrock. When it cooled, the rock crystallized into these regular formations, but it would be easy to believe that the blocks were stacked by some giant hand, driven on in its monumental task by the force of some great purpose.

This, of course, is what the ancient Irish believed and who else could have completed the task but the legendary giant Finn McCool, the Ulster warrior who was said to inhabit this Antrim headland? When he once scooped up a clod of earth to throw at a rival, the place he took it from filled with water to become Lough Neagh, the largest lake in the British Isles, and the clod landed in the Irish sea

and became the Isle of Man. According to legend, he built the Causeway so that he could cross the sea to reach the lady giant of his dreams, who lived on Staffa – a tall story in more ways than one.

The reality is equally remarkable, but whatever created the Causeway, it is a magnificent sight, particularly when approached on foot from above. There is a cliff-top path all along this stretch of coastline, which can be joined at Blackrock, 2.5km (1.5 miles) from Causeway Head, or from the **Causeway Visitor Centre.**

The Visitor Centre is on the cliff top and is a good introduction to the site. It includes an audio-visual theatre, where a 25-minute show tells the story of the formation of the Causeway. There is also an exhibition area with displays including birdlife and the legend of Finn McCool. A minibus runs from here to the Causeway at regular intervals in the summer and guided tours are available.

Beside the centre is the **Causeway School Museum,** a reconstructed 1920s schoolroom complete with learning aids and toys of the era.

🚼 9A 🚌 172 Ballycastle–Portrush; summer services 177 from Coleraine and 252 from Belfast and Larne 🚉 Portrush (11km/7 miles)

Causeway Visitor Centre

✉ 44 Causeway Road, Bushmills ☎ 028 2073 1855
🕐 Daily 10–5 (closes 7pm Jul–Aug, 4:30pm Nov–Feb)
✋ Free. Moderate charge for parking and extra charge for audio-visual theatre 🍴 Tea room (€)

Causeway School Museum

✉ 52 Causeway Road, Bushmills ☎ 028 2073 1777
🕐 Jul–Aug daily 11–5 ✋ Inexpensive

5 Kilkenny

Narrow medieval streets and alleys linking the great castle and cathedral bear witness to Kilkenny's rich history and architectural heritage.

Standing on a bend of the River Nore, Kilkenny is one of Ireland's most beautiful towns, with pretty little streets to explore, high quality craft studios and an exceptional range of historic buildings.

In medieval times, the town rivalled Dublin in importance and the great **castle** here was the stronghold of the most powerful family in Ireland at the time, the Butlers, Earls and Dukes of Ormonde. Though its origins are back in Norman times, the castle was adapted over the centuries and now reflects the splendour of the 1830s, enhanced by the Butler Gallery of Contemporary Art in the former servants' quarters, the Medieval Room in the South Tower and a cultural facility.

Opposite the castle is the **Kilkenny Design Centre** (► 108), which was established in the 1960s to bring Irish craftsmanship to new heights of excellence. Not only was the centre resoundingly successful, it became the spearhead of a crafts revival that has attracted fine craft workers from all over the world. **Rothe House,** a Tudor mansion on three sides of a cobbled courtyard, is also worth a visit. Here you'll find a range of restored rooms, the city and county museum and a costume collection.

Kilkenny originally grew up around the 6th-century monastery founded by St Canice, to whom the cathedral is dedicated. Built on the site of the original monastery, it remains one of the finest 13th-century buildings in Ireland and contains

impressive monuments of black Kilkenny marble and the Cityscope Exhibition. Beside the cathedral is the well-preserved round tower of the original monastery, which gives great views over the city.

✚ 20J 🚉 Kilkenny 1.5km (1 mile)

ℹ Shee Alms House, Rose Inn Street ☎ 056-775 1500

Kilkenny Castle
✉ The Parade ☎ 056-772 1450; www.heritageireland.ie
🕐 Jun–Sep daily 10–7; Apr–May daily 10:30–5; Oct–Mar Tue–Sat 10:30–12:45, 2–5, Sun 10–7 (guided tours only)
🖐 Moderate 🍴 Tea room May–Sep (€)

Kilkenny Design Centre
✉ Castle Yard ☎ 056-772 2118; www.kilkennydesign.com
🕐 Apr–Dec Mon–Sat 9–6, Sun 10–6; Jan–Mar Mon–Sat 9–6 🍴 Restaurant (€)

Rothe House
✉ Parliament Street ☎ 056-772 2893 🕐 Apr–Oct Mon–Sat 10:30–5, Sun 3–5; Nov–Mar Mon–Sat 10:30–4
🖐 Moderate

6 Muckross House

www.muckross-house.ie

Among Ireland's foremost stately homes, Muckross has folk and farm museums and beautiful gardens – all within the Killarney National Park.

When Henry Arthur Herbert, Member of Parliament for Co Kerry, built his Elizabethan-style mansion in 1843, he could not have found a more perfect site, looking out towards Muckross Lake and surrounded by wonderful scenery that was destined to become a national park. Maud Bowers Bourne was given the house as a wedding present in 1911. Her family presented the house and estate to the Irish nation in 1932 in her memory.

While the house sums up the lifestyle of the landed gentry in Victorian times, the servants' quarters have been converted into a museum of Kerry folk life, with displays and a weaver's workshop. The Muckross Craft Centre features weaving, pottery and bookbinding workshops. There is also a restaurant and gift shop. Out in the grounds, a 28ha (69-acre) farm has been constructed to show farming methods that were used before mechanization. The rare Kerry cow, a small, black, hardy animal, is being bred here in order to save the herd from extinction.

The gardens at Muckross are renowned for their beauty. Many tender and exotic species thrive in the mild climate, and there are lovely water and rock gardens. A number of nature trails of various lengths begin here, from a one-hour stroll to a 16km (10-mile) circular Heritage Trail through the most extensive natural yew woods in Europe.

✠ 15L ✉ 5km (3 miles) south of Killarney ☎ 064-31440 ⊛ House and Gardens: Jul–Aug daily 9–6; Sep–Jun daily 9–5:30. Farm: Mar–Apr, Oct Sat–Sun 1–6; May daily 1–6; Jun–Sep daily 10–6 ✋ House and Farm expensive; House moderate; Gardens free ⑪ Cafe (€) 🚌 From Killarney ❓ Horse-drawn jaunting cars from Killarney to the house

7

The National Museum, Dublin

www.museum.ie

Three locations in Dublin house the magnificent and varied collections and priceless treasures of the National Museum.

The oldest of the trio (1857) is the Natural History Museum, Merrion Street, which has one of the finest zoological collections in the world. The ground floor has collections relating to native Irish wildlife, while the upper floor has the World Collection, with many African and Asian species, all overlooked by the skeleton of a 20m (65ft)

whale. Here, too, is a wonderful collection of glass reproductions of marine specimens.

The Kildare Street branch houses the archaeological collections. The centrepiece is a glittering display of ancient gold dating from around 2200 to 700BC. Some of the gold has faint traces of Celtic decoration, but the best examples of this are to be found in the National Treasury in the adjacent room. Some of the patterns, worked in silver and gold many centuries ago, are almost too tiny to be appreciated by the naked eye. There is a huge collection of Viking artefacts, many found during the redevelopment of Wood Quay. The Road to Independence is an evocative exhibition featuring the events and consequences of the Easter Rising and the Civil War.

Across the city, on the north bank of the River Liffey, the restored Collins Barracks house the National Museum's collection of decorative arts, and displays relating to social, political and military history. These include costumes and jewellery, weaponry and furniture, silver, ceramics and glassware, and interactive multimedia terminals provide more interpretation. There is also an interesting section explaining how the museum goes about the process of research, restoration and conservation of its treasures.

🞧 *Dublin 8e, Dublin 1c (Collins Barracks)* ✉ Kildare Street, Merrion Street, Benburb Street ☎ 01-677 7444 🕘 Tue–Sat 10–5, Sun 2–5 🎫 Free 🍴 Cafés at Kildare Street and Collins Barracks (€) 🚌 Cross-city buses 🚉 Pearse station 5-min walk; Heuston Station for Collins Barracks ❓ Guided tours depart from the main entrance at regular intervals

8 Oileáin Árann (Aran Islands)

Bleak and virtually treeless, these three remote islands on the very edge of Europe have a fascinating cultural heritage.

From the mainland, the distant sight of the three Aran Islands is mysterious and inviting. The west coast of Ireland may seem a remote outpost of Europe, and yet here is something beyond – a place where Gaelic is still the first language, old traditions live on and a small population still scratches a living from the often inhospitable land. Summer visitors are important to the economy, as is the sale of Aran knitwear.

Of the three islands – Inis Mór (Inishmore), Inis Meáin (Inishmaan) and Inis Oírr (Inisheer) – Inis Mór is the largest, and Cill Rónáin (Kilronan) is its main settlement. **Aran's Heritage Centre,** with exhibitions, crafts and an audio-visual show, will steer you towards the many attractions of the islands, from their wonderful beaches to the plentiful historic sites.

There is evidence of prehistoric settlement on the islands. Inis Mór has no fewer than five stone forts, including the dramatic Dún Aonghasa, perched above a 91m (298ft) drop to the sea, and Dún Eochla on the island's highest point.

More atmospheric still are the early Christian sites. The islands have a number of ancient

churches, including Teampall Bheanáin, which was
built in the 6th century, and Teampall Chiaráin,
dating from the 8th or 9th centuries.

The islands deserve more than just a day trip,
which can only scratch the surface of what they
have to offer.

✚ 15G 🚍 No public transport on the islands ✈ Aer Arann
(☎ 091-593034; www.aerarannislands.ie) operates flights
taking 10 minutes from Connemara Airport,
Co Galway. May–Aug every 30 mins (last flight 7pm);
Sep–Apr less frequent 🚢 Island Ferries (☎ 091-568903;
www.aranislandferries.com) operates several sailings daily
from Rossaveal, Co Galway

Aran's Heritage Centre
✉ Kilronan, Inis Mór ☎ 099-61355 🕐 Jun–Aug daily 10–7;
Apr–May, Sep–Oct daily 11–5 🎫 Inexpensive

The Rock of Cashel

Ancient seat of the kings of Munster and a medieval religious centre, the Rock of Cashel is an awe-inspiring sight.

This single craggy hill, rising out of the surrounding plain and topped by a cluster of wonderful medieval buildings, dominates the skyline. It is a great landmark that draws more than the eye – its romantic outline of ruined towers and graceful arches seems to beckon from a distance.

The great rock was the obvious choice as the fortress of the kings of Munster, who ruled the southern part of Ireland, and Cashel came to prominence in the 4th or 5th century AD. Legend has it that St Patrick came here to baptize the king, and that during the ceremony, the saint accidentally

drove the sharp end of his crozier through the king's foot. The king bore the pain unflinchingly because he believed it to be part of the initiation.

The dominant building on the rock is the 13th-century St Patrick's Cathedral, roofless now, but still impressive, with its long nave and chancel and a 26m (85ft) tower. Inside is a wealth of monuments, including important tombs, and the west end is formed by a 15th-century castle, built as the Archbishop's residence.

The Round Tower and Cormac's Chapel are the oldest structures on the Rock, dating from the 11th to 12th centuries, and the chapel contains a remarkable stone sarcophagus carved with sophisticated Celtic patterns. One of the later buildings, the 15th-century Hall of the Vicars, is one of the first you see on the Rock, with a display of stone carvings in its vaulted undercroft and above it a splendid hall with a minstrels' gallery, huge fireplace and wonderful timbered ceiling.

✚ 19J ✉ Rock of Cashel ☎ 062-61437; www.heritageireland.ie 🕐 Mid-Mar to mid-Jun daily 9:30–5:30; mid-Jun to mid-Sep daily 9–7; mid-Sep to mid-Oct daily 9–5:30; mid-Oct to mid-Mar daily 9–4:30 💷 Moderate 🚌 Dublin–Cork buses ❓ Guided tours on request. Audio-visual, Jun–Sep

10 Ulster-American Folk Park

www.folkpark.com

The lives and experiences of Ulster emigrants to the New World are authentically recreated at this splendid open-air museum.

In a great tide of emigration during the 18th and 19th centuries, over 2 million people left Ulster for a different life in the New World. Among them was five-year-old Thomas Mellon, who went on to become a judge and founder of the Pittsburgh dynasty of bankers, and it is around his childhood home that this museum has been created. Buildings have been reconstructed on the site, giving a complete picture of the world that the emigrants left behind and the one that was awaiting them on the other side of the Atlantic.

The Ulster section includes a typical one-room cottage of the late 18th century, a forge and weaver's cottage, schoolhouse and post office, places of worship and a 19th-century street of shops, with original Victorian shopfronts. Houses include the boyhood homes of John Joseph Hughes, the first Roman Catholic Archbishop of New York, and Robert Campbell, who became a fur trader in the Rockies and a successful merchant in St Louis.

On the dockside, you can see a typical merchant's office and a boarding house where

emigrants would await their sailing, then board a reconstruction of the kind of sailing ship which carried them to their new lives.

Beyond this you emerge into the American section of the park, with log houses and barns, including a replica of the six-roomed farmhouse that Thomas Mellon's father built. The buildings contain over 2,000 19th-century artefacts collected in Pennsylvania and Virginia.

✠ 8C ✉ 2 Mellon Road, Castletown ☎ 028 8224 3292 🕐 Apr–Sep Mon–Sat 10:30–6, Sun and public hols 11–6; Oct–Mar Mon–Fri 10:30–5. Last admission 90 mins before closing ♿ Moderate 🍴 Cafe (€) 🚌 273 Belfast–Londonderry ❓ Special events to celebrate the Ulster-American connection are held throughout the year. Special celebrations on Independence Day, 4 July

Best things to do

Good places to have lunch

Ahernes (€€–€€€)
Ahernes has a world reputation for its fine seafood dishes.
✉ 163 North Main Street, Youghal, Co Cork ☎ 024-92424

Ballymaloe House (€€)
Here, at the home of the Ballymaloe Cookery School, local produce is used to produce excellent, good-value food.
✉ Shanagarry Midleton, Co Cork ☎ 021-465 2531

Eccles Hotel (€€)
Charming Victorian hotel, where good food can be enjoyed while overlooking Bantry Bay.
✉ Glengarriff, Co Cork ☎ 027-63003

The Edge (€€)
Feast on delectable dishes prepared with local produce, while

enjoying panoramic views over the River Lagan.

✉ Mays Meadow, Laganbank Road, Belfast ☎ 028 9032 2000

Gruel (€–€€)

Rustic little eatery in the middle of Dublin city centre. French peasant-inspired menu with adventurous Irish touches.

✉ 68a Dame Street, Dublin 2 ☎ 01-670 7119

Harvey's Point (€€)

Great food in a wonderful location on the edge of Lough Eske.

✉ Lough Eske, Donegal ☎ 074-972 2208

Nick's Warehouse (£–££)

Superb food in a popular, modern venue. The daily changing menu is dedicated to local and organic producers and there is an excellent wine list.

✉ 35–39 Hill Street, Belfast ☎ 028 9043 9690

Paddy Burke's (€€)

Paddy Burke's is famous as the focal point of the popular Clarenbridge Oyster Festival, so it is not surprising that its speciality dish is shellfish.

✉ Clarenbridge, Co Galway ☎ 091-796226

Patrick Guilbaud (€€€)

One of the finest restaurants in the city offering superb classic French cuisine in elegant surroundings, featuring a fine collection of Irish art. Popular with business clients.

✉ 21 Upper Merrion Street, Dublin ☎ 01-676 4192

Ramore Wine Bar (£–££)

A popular restaurant right on the harbour, offering excellent food and a good wine list.

✉ The Harbour, Portrush, Co Antrim ☎ 028 7082 4313

Best castles

Ballynahinch Castle, Co Galway Stunning 18th-century country house on the banks of the River Owenmore.

Carrickfergus Castle, Co Antrim Built in 1180, this was one of the first, and largest, of the Irish castles, and is still in good condition (➤ 168).

Castle Leslie, Co Monaghan Winston Churchill, W B Yeats, Paul MaCartney – they have all fallen for the charms of this 1870 palace, now a hotel, on the shores of Glaslough Lake.

Dublin Castle, Dublin For centuries the seat of British rule in Ireland, this stern castle sits in the heart of the capital and houses the fabulous Chester Beatty Library (➤ 82).

Glin Castle, Co Limerick If you're into 17th- and 18th-century Irish decorative arts, neo-Gothic Glin Castle is the place to head for.

Johnstown Castle, Co Wexford This Gothic Revival extravaganza was built at the heart of some magnificent parkland (➤ 99).

Kilkenny Castle, Co Kilkenny Gothic and Victorian styles meet in this pristine, grey-stone castle on the banks of the River Nore in Kilkenny City (➤ 44–45).

Lismore Castle, Co Waterford This vast, turreted, grey-stone building tops a rock that overhangs the Blackwater River.

Slane Castle, Co Meath More stately home than granite fortress, 18th-century Slane Castle overlooks a natural amphitheatre.

Tullynally Castle, Co Westmeath
The largest Irish castle still functioning as a family home. The real joy here is the beautiful gardens and parkland that surround it.

Stunning scenery

Top activities

Angling: Ireland is one of the outstanding angling destinations in Europe. There are opportunities for beginners and experts alike and information on all aspects of angling can be found on the website of **Central Fisheries Board** at www.cfb.ie

Birdwatching: With over 420 species of birds recorded in Ireland and wonderfully diverse habitats there is plenty for the avid birdwatcher to see. Eric Dempsey, an Irish Tourist Board (Faílte Ireland) approved guide, runs a variety of birding tours throughout the country. Check out his website for all the details at www.birdsireland.com

Cruising on the Shannon or Erne waterways: Try your hand at inland cruising by taking out a small boat, then pulling up at a pub at night. Most of the length of the River Shannon is navigable and the Shannon–Erne Waterway links the river to Lough Erne.

Cycling: Ireland is a great place to get on your bicycle, with quiet rural roads and some spectacular mountain and coastal rides. The west and southwest are particularly good for cycling routes.

Gaelic sports: The Irish are passionate about their traditional sports. The most watched sporting event in Ireland is the Gaelic football All-Ireland final held in September in Dublin. The game is very fast, a cross between rugby and football. Hurling is specific to Ireland and is popular everywhere.
Gaelic Athletic Association (GAA) ✉ Pairc an Chrocaigh, Dublin 3
☎ 01-836 3222 ✉ Belfast ☎ 028 3752 1907

Golf: There are over 400 golf courses in Ireland. The Republic of Ireland's golfing body can give details on all of Ireland's courses.
Golfing Union of Ireland ✉ Carton Demesne, Maynooth, Co Kildare
☎ 01-505 4000; www.gui.ie

Horse-back riding: The affinity between the Irish and horses is legendary, and there are hundreds of places around the country where you can enjoy lovely scenery on horseback.
Association of Irish Riding Establishments (AIRE) ✉ TiBroin, Kiltimon, Ashford, Co Wicklow ☎ 01-281 0963; www.aire.ie

Horse racing: This is very popular in the Republic of Ireland. There are 27 racecourses, and races are held nearly every day.
Horse Racing Ireland ☎ 045-455455; www.goracing.ie

Sailing: You'd be hard pushed to find a part of Ireland's coastline where there isn't a local sailing club nearby.
Irish Sailing Association – check out www.sailing.ie to locate a club.

Walking: Every region of Ireland offers great walking opportunities and the local tourist offices have information for area hikes. Some towns celebrate with annual walking festivals, such as the one in Kenmare, Co Kerry, in late May.

Boat trips

One of the best ways to see the diversity of coast, island and river scenery is to go on a boat trip. Contact the booking offices of the following companies directly or check with the local tourist office. Most trips are May to October only.

Báan Daingin (Dingle Bay) and Fungi the Dolphin (Dingle Bay Ferries, Dunromen, Lispole, Co Kerry ☎ 066-915 0768)

Cork Harbour from Cobh (Marine Transport Services, Westland House, Rushbrooke, Cobh ☎ 021-481 1549)

Killarney Lakes from Ross Castle (Killarney Watercoach Cruises, Old Weir Lodge, Killarney, Co Kerry ☎ 064-35593)

Lough Corrib and Inchagoill Island (Tourist office, Eyre Square, Galway ☎ 091-537700)

Lough Derg–Killaloe (Derg Maine, Kilaloe, Co Clare ☎ 061-376364)

Lough Key Forest Park (Lough Key Boat Tours, Rockingham Harbour, Lough Key Forest Park, Boyle, Co Roscommon ☎ 086-816 7637)

Lough Ree–Athlone (Athlone Cruiser, Jolly Mariner, Maine, Athlone, Co Westmeath ☎ 090-647 2892)

River Erne from Belturbet (Emerald Star, Belturbet, Co Cavan ☎ 071-962 7633)

Skelligs from Valencia (The Skellig Experience, Valencia Island, Co Kerry ☎ 066-947 6306)

Waterford–Carrick-on-Suir Castle (Gallery Cruising Restaurant, Bridge Quay, New Ross, Co Wexford ☎ 051-421723)

Best souvenirs

Aran knitwear – the distinctive patterns of the traditional Aran sweater are known all over the world. They are still produced in the Oileáin Árann (Aran Islands).

Belleek pottery – the famous basket-weave pottery has been made at the west end of Loch Erne in Co Fermanagh since 1857 and the same traditional methods are still employed. Take a tour of the factory and you can see the craftspeople at work, then visit the vistor's centre and shop.

Claddagh rings – found in shops throughout Ireland, traditional Celtic designs are popular, in particular the Claddagh ring, a design dating from the 17th century. The ring consists of a heart encircled by a pair of hands with a crown above the heart. It symbolizes love and fidelity.

Connemara marble – it has been quarried in Connemara for centuries and you can buy a huge range of items, from massive kitchen worktops to delicate rosary beads and jewellery. Check out Connemara Marble Industries in Moycullen.

Donegal tweed – Magee & Co in Donegal town have been manufacturing tweed since 1866. Ardara Heritage Centre tells the story of Donegal tweed and Aran knitwear, and there are tours of hand-loom weaving centres.

Irish drinks – choose from Bushmills, Jameson, Powers and Paddy whiskeys; Guinness, Beamish and Murphy's stout; Smithwick's beer; Cork gin; and Bailey's liqueur. Take a tour of the Guinness Storehouse (► 84–85) or the Old Jameson Distillery (► 87) in Dublin, the Old Bushmills Distillery in Co Antrim or the Jameson Heritage Centre in Midleton, Co Cork.

Irish lace – lace-making today is big business, with large factories producing fabric in minutes, but it all stems from a cottage industry and some is still handmade today. Take your pick of local lace. The famous names include Limerick, Kenmare, Youghal and Carrickmacross.

Irish linen – Banbridge, Co Down is the main centre. The Ferguson Linen Centre has factory tours, and Banbridge is the starting point of Linen Tours, a coach journey around nearby sites, including linen mills and factories. There is also an Irish Linen Centre in Lisburn.

Peat carvings – a unique souvenir crafted from 5,000-year-old Irish turf from some of Ireland's oldest boglands. Choose from jewellery in traditional Celtic designs, clocks, paperweights and more. One producer is Island Turf Crafts in Coalisland, Co Tyrone.

Waterford crystal – founded in 1783, the business is now a highly commercial operation, but it is still made in the same town and by much the same method as when it was first set up. The factory on the outskirts of Waterford has organized tours (► 128).

Places to take the children

BALLYPOREEN, CO TIPPERARY
Mitchelstown Caves
The caves are renowned for their depth of 1km (half a mile), and comprise two groups, Desmond's Cave and New Cave.
✉ Off the N8, 4km (2.5 miles) north of Ballyporeen ☎ 052-67246
⏰ Feb–Sep daily 10–5:30; Oct–Jan daily 10:30–5 ✋ Moderate

BELFAST
Belfast Zoo
A modern world-class zoo set in attractive parkland and housing over 160 species of rare and endangered animals.
✉ Off Antrim Road ☎ 028 9077 6277; www.belfastzoo.co.uk ⏰ Apr–Sep daily 10–5; Oct–Mar daily 10–2:30 ✋ Moderate 🍴 Refreshments (£)

W5
An interactive discovery centre located at the Odyssey in central Belfast. There are five exhibition areas: Wow, Start, Go, See and Do.
✉ 2 Queen's Quay ☎ 028 9046 7700; www.w5online.co.uk ⏰ Sep–Jun Mon–Thu 10–4, Fri–Sat 10–5, Sun 12–5; Jul–Aug daily 10–5 ✋ Moderate

DINGLE, CO KERRY
Dingle Oceanworld
Underwater life galore. Watch out for the sharks!
✉ Dingle Harbour ☎ 066-915 2111 ⏰ Phone for opening times
✋ Expensive

DUBLIN
Dublin Zoo
This historic zoo in Phoenix Park makes an ideal family day out.
✉ Phoenix Park ☎ 01-474 8900; www.dublinzoo.ie ⏰ Mar–Sep Mon–Sat 9:30–6, Sun 10:30–6; Oct–Feb Mon–Sat 9:30–dusk, Sun 10:30–dusk
✋ Expensive 🍴 Restaurant and cafés (€–€€)

Viking Splash Tour

Take a tour of Dublin in an ex-World War II amphibious vehicle. It takes in all the main city-centre sights – then heads straight into the waters of Grand Canal Basin to finish the tour afloat.

✉ 64–65 Patrick Street ☎ 01-707 6000; www.vikingsplash.ie ⏰ Every half hour 10–12, 1:30–5. Mar–Oct daily; Feb Wed–Sun; Nov Tue–Sun ✋ Expensive

FOTA, CO CORK
Fota Wildlife Park

Established by the Royal Zoological Society of Ireland, Fota Wildlife Park's primary aim is the breeding of endangered species.

✉ 1.5km (1 mile) south of Cork Harbour ☎ 021-481 2678; www.fotawildlife.ie ⏰ Mon–Sat 10–4:30, Sun 11–4:30 ✋ Expensive

SALTHILL, CO GALWAY
Leisureland

A modern pool complex with waterslides, treasure cove, tropical beach pool and playground.

☎ 091-521455 ⏰ Mon–Fri 8am–10pm, Sat 8–5, Sun 8–6 ✋ Moderate

SHANNONBRIDGE
Clonmacnoise & West Offaly Railway

Narrow-gauge railway tour of the Blackwater bog (9km/5.5 miles) with on-board commentary.

☎ 090-967 4114 ⏰ Apr–May, Sep Mon–Fri 10–5; Jun–Aug daily 10–5, trains leave on the hour. Groups only in winter ✋ Moderate 🍴 Coffee shop (€)

TRALEE, CO KERRY
Aqua Dome

Tralee's wonderful waterpark has all the rides you would expect. You can also visit the Blennerville Windmill.

✉ On the Dingle road ☎ Aqua Dome: 066-712 8899 ⏰ Aqua Dome Mon–Fri 10–10, Sat–Sun 11–8; windmill Apr–Oct 10–6 ✋ Expensive

Traditional music

Some of the best traditional music nights are the impromptu sessions in local pubs throughout Ireland. Check at the tourist offices for what's likely to be on where. Here are just a few suggestions.

An Daingean (Dingle) – a wealth of musical talent can be heard in this area of western Ireland. Among many popular venues in the town are An Chonair, An Droichead, McCarthy's Pub and the Marina Inn.

Belfast – the John Hewitt Bar in Donegall Street hosts regular traditional music sessions, as well as some nights of jazz. Good food and great for conversation with no television, taped music, juke box or gaming machines.

Cork – try the Lobby Bar in Union Quay and the Old Oak Bar in Oliver Plunkett Street.

Doolin – hot spot in Co Clare for some great music with O'Connor's a favourite. Most of the great names have played here and it has become a bit of an institution. But don't be afraid to sing along – it's a jolly place to go. McGann's, by the bridge, is a quieter, more serious venue.

Dublin – for a bit of musical history go to O'Donoghue's in Merrion Row. Here the music is spontaneous and lively. It's a small venue which gets very crowded and it's where the famous Dubliners folk group started their career back in the early 1960s. The Cobblestone in Smithfield is an authentic and popular venue for traditional music every night of the week.

Galway – continuing western Ireland's tradition for great sounds, try Tigh Neachtain in Cross Street.

Howth – just to the north of Dublin and a short trip on the DART, you'll find traditional music in this popular fishing village at the Abbey Tavern.

Kenmare – there's a great tradition of good Irish music in this attractive little town in Co Kerry. For the closest to the real thing try Crowley's in Henry Street for the best in impromptu sessions. You can find more in the smart surroundings of the Landsdowne Arms Hotel.

Sligo – another area known for good traditional music in both the town and local villages – check with the tourist office for venues. Furey's in Sligo is owned by the traditional band Dervish and is worth a visit.

Westport – in Co Mayo, popular for its traditional music, you will find Matt Molloy's, owned by Molloy, the flute player of the world-famous folk band the Chieftains, who still often plays here.

a walk

around Dublin

This walk starts in Dublin's most famous shopping street, then takes in many of the city's major attractions.

Walk south along Grafton Street, cross the road and enter the gardens of St Stephen's Green, leaving by the small gate at the left corner. Cross the road and go forward along Kildare Street.

The National Museum, on the right, is Ireland's treasure house, with some stunning objects and fascinating exhibitions (➤ 48–49).

At the end of Kildare Street go left into Nassau Street, then right to College Green, with Trinity College on the right (➤ 88–89). Follow Westmoreland Street, walk

across O'Connell Bridge and turn left alongside the river. Cross Ha'penny Bridge (footbridge), then go through Merchant's Arch into Temple Bar (▶ 88).

This network of cobbled lanes is worth exploring.

Turn right into Essex Street East. Take the third left into Eustace Street. At the end turn right along Dame Street.

Dublin Castle is on the left, its medieval origins buried beneath 18th-century reconstructions that house the truly magnificent State Apartments, including the Throne Room (▶ 82).

Keep forward to Christ Church Cathedral.

Begun in the 12th century, beautiful Christ Church is the foremost cathedral in Dublin. Next to it is Dvblinia (▶ 84).

Go down Fishamble Street to the river. Turn right along the south bank, and at O'Connell Bridge turn right and return to Grafton Street.

Distance About 4km (2.5 miles)
Time 3–4 hours
Start/end point Grafton Street 🚇 *Dublin 7e*
Lunch The Auld Dubliner (€) ✉ 24–25 Temple Bar ☎ 01- 677 0527

Following the literary greats

Samuel Beckett (1906–1989) – the author and playwright, born and educated in Dublin, was one-time associate and assistant to James Joyce. His play *Waiting for Godot* is probably his most well-known work.

Seamus Heaney (born 1939) – this Nobel-prize-winning poet, born in Mossbawn, Co Londonderry, and a graduate of Queen's University, Belfast, went on to be a professor at both Harvard and Oxford universities.

James Joyce (1882–1941) – probably the most famous of them all. You can follow his trail throughout Dublin City and there's a day dedicated to his most well-known hero Leopold Bloom, immortalized in *Ulysses*. You will find his statue in Earl Street.

Patrick Kavanagh (1904–1967) – the poet was born near Inniskeen, Co Monaghan. Sit next to him on a bench by the Grand Canal in Dublin where he meditates in bronze.

Edna O'Brien (born 1936) – gained her insight into the repressive position of women in Irish society from her early days in the rural Catholic village of Tuamgraney in Co Clare.

George Bernard Shaw (1856–1950) – 'author of many plays' is the simple accolade on the plaque outside Shaw's Birthplace in Synge Street, close to the Grand Canal in Dublin.

Bram Stoker (1847–1912) – the author of the classic Gothic horror tale, *Dracula*, lived and worked in Dublin,

running the Lyceum Theatre in conjunction with the actor
Henry Irving.

Jonathan Swift (1667–1745) – a Dublin man born and bred and
later to become dean of St Patrick's Cathedral, Swift is probably
best known for his satirical work *Gulliver's Travels*.

Oscar Wilde (1854–1900) – born in Dublin. You can visit his house,
and be sure not to miss his wonderful reclining statue in nearby
Merrion Square.

W B Yeats (1865–1939) – although born in Dublin, Yeats has
connections with other parts of Ireland. He lived for a time at
Thor Ballylee Tower south of Galway and there is an impressive
statue of him (► opposite) in the town of Sligo, which hosts an
annual Yeats summer school.

Exploring

It's the diverse nature of Ireland that lives in the memory. From vibrant, cosmopolitan cities to quiet rural backwaters; from coast to mountains; from picture postcard villages to market towns – the country and its people are unique. If you have only time to visit Dublin, at least try and take a trip on the DART; in a few minutes you will be along the coast, adding a further dimension to your visit. As in so many countries, the cities are only part of the whole and not a true reflection of the country. You won't go anywhere very fast, although the roads have improved dramatically, but that is part of the charm. People don't rush in Ireland and even in Dublin and Belfast, now cities competing with any other major European destination for culture, restaurants and vibrant nightlife, the locals still have time to stop and chat.

The East

The eastern part of Ireland is inevitably dominated by Dublin, a lively city with a lot to see and do, but the east has much more to offer than just the capital. Ireland's most extensive mountain region is just to the south of Dublin in Co Wicklow, where remote, silent valleys and wild exposed mountain tops can be reached in less than half an hour's drive.

Long sandy beaches and golf links stretch along the coast, which remains unspoiled in spite of the presence of the main ferry ports. The resorts retain an old-fashioned appeal.

Inland, the east has some fascinating places to see. To the north of Dublin is a cluster of historic sites including Tara, Kells and Newgrange. Southwest of the capital is the horse-racing centre of Kildare and The Curragh and the wonderful old city of Kilkenny, and in the far south are the pretty villages and fine beaches of the Wexford coast.

DUBLIN

Part of Dublin's charm is that it takes only a few days of wandering around its attractive streets and leafy squares to feel you know the city intimately. And yet, every visit reveals some new delight.

Dublin has everything a capital city should have – magnificent architecture, excellent shopping, lively entertainment and cultural events, superb museums and galleries, colourful parks and gardens and a strong sense of history.

Until now, most of Dublin's attractions have been in the smart areas south of the river. The northside was once a run-down area with seedy back streets, but now a redevelopment plan has given it the designer treatment. Wide O'Connell Street has become an attractive, leafy boulevard; behind it in Henry Street the shopping centres have been upgraded and the area now rivals Grafton Street. Smithfield Village is taking shape as an interesting cultural quarter to match the already rejuvenated Temple Bar, which has continued to grow. The docks are being developed and the new LUAS light rail system brings Dubliners in from the suburbs.

✚ 22G

ℹ Suffolk Street ☎ 01-605 7700

Dublin Castle

Soon after the Anglo-Normans arrived in Ireland in the 12th century, King John ordered the building of Dublin Castle and it remained the centre of English power in Ireland until 1922. In spite of its great medieval walls and round bastions, much of the castle is a product of the 18th century, including the State Apartments, where presidents are inaugurated and dignitaries received. The Chester Beatty Library, one of the world's best collections of Oriental and European manuscripts, is located in the castle gardens.

www.dublincastle.ie

✚ *Dublin 5e* ✉ Dame Street ☎ 01-677 7129 🕐 Mon–Fri 10–4:45, Sat–Sun, public hols 2–4:45 (State Apartments may be closed for functions) ✋ Free. State Apartments tour moderate 🍴 Restaurant (€) 🚌 Cross-city buses

Dublin Writers Museum

No other city in the world has spawned so many writers of international repute, including four Nobel prize winners, and this museum is a celebration of that literary heritage. The displays, in the magnificent surroundings of a restored 18th-century mansion, encompass the whole spectrum of Irish works, from the 8th-century *Book of Kells* to the present, taking in Swift, Sheridan, Shaw, Wilde, Yeats, Joyce and Beckett along the way.

One room is devoted entirely to children's literature, and there are regular exhibitions and readings.

www.writersmuseum.com

✚ *Dublin 6a* ✉ 18–19 Parnell Square North ☎ 01-872 2077 🕐 Mon–Sat 10–5 (until 6pm Mon–Fri Jun–Aug), Sun and public hols 11–5 💷 Moderate 🍴 Restaurant (€€) and coffee shop (€) 🚌 10, 11, 11a, 11b, 13, 16a, 19a, 22, 22A, 36 🚆 DART and LUAS: Connolly

Dvblinia and the Viking World

Developed by the Medieval Trust, Dvblinia tells the story of the city from the arrival of the Anglo-Normans in the 12th century until the closure of the monasteries in 1540. It is housed in a beautifully preserved old building, the former Synod Hall, linked to Christ Church Cathedral by an ancient covered bridge. The 'Viking World' exhibition reconstructs life in even earlier Viking Dublin.
www.dublinia.ie

➕ *Dublin 4e* ✉ St Michael's Hill ☎ 01-679 4611 🕐 Apr–Sep daily 10–5; Oct–Mar Mon–Fri 11–4, Sat–Sun and public hols 10–4 ✋ Moderate 🍴 Tea rooms Jun–Aug (€) 🚌 51b, 78a, 90, 123

Guinness Storehouse

Guinness, one of the most potent symbols of Irishness, is now brewed all over the world – at a rate of over 10 million glasses a day – and this is where it all started, founded by Arthur Guinness in

1759. As you enter the Storehouse through a stone arch an escalator whisks you to the heart of the building into what is described as a large glass pint. Within this glass structure you journey through the production process. Entertaining displays and audio-visuals give an insight into the history, manufacturing and advertising of Dublin's most famous product. You will end your visit in the glass-walled rooftop bar where you can sample a free glass of the 'black stuff'.

www.guinnessstorehouse.com

✚ *Dublin 1e* ✉ St James's Gate ☎ 01-404 4800 🕐 Daily 9:30–5, (until 8pm Jul–Aug) 💷 Expensive 🍴 Brewery bar, Gravity bar 🚌 51b, 78a from Aston Quay; 123 from O'Connell Street. LUAS: James Street

Kilmainham Gaol

In its time both a caution and an inspiration, Kilmainham Gaol stands as a monument to the struggle for Irish independence and those leaders of the 1916 Easter Rising who were imprisoned or executed here. It gives visitors a chillingly realistic impression of what life must have been like for the prisoners who were incarcerated here, be they patriots or petty criminals, from its inauguration in 1796 to 1924.

✚ *Dublin 1d (off map)* ✉ Inchicore Road, Kilmainham ☎ 01-453 5984; www.heritageireland.ie 🕐 Apr–Sep daily 9:30–5; Oct–Mar Mon–Sat 9:30–4, Sun 10–5 💷 Moderate 🚌 51B, 78A, 79 from Aston Quay. LUAS: Museum Stop 🚆 Heuston Station

National Gallery of Ireland

First opened in 1864, this wonderful gallery has one of the finest collections of European art in the world. Located in the heart of Georgian Dublin, the gallery contains nearly 2,500 paintings, over 5,000 drawings, watercolours and miniatures, over 3,000 prints and more than 300 pieces of sculpture and *objets d'art*. The Millennium Wing houses a centre for the study of Irish art and an archive dedicated to the paintings of Jack B Yeats (1872–1957).

www.nationalgallery.ie

🚩 *Dublin 8e* 📧 Merrion Square West and Clare Street ☎ 01-661 5133
🕐 Mon–Wed, Fri–Sat 9:30–5:30, Thu 9–8:30, Sun 2–5:30. Closed Good Fri, 24–26 Dec 🖐 Voluntary 🍴 Restaurant and café (€€) 🚌 Cross-city buses
🚉 DART Pearse

National Museum
Best places to see, ➤ 48–49.

Old Jameson Distillery
Explore the history of Irish whiskey-making, which goes back to the 6th century, through exhibits and audio-visual presentations on the site of the old Jameson Distillery in Smithfield Village, on the north side of the River Liffey. You can view old and new equipment and watch a working bottling line, then sample a drop of the *uisce beatha*, literally 'water of life'. There is an excellent shop selling a variety of whiskies, as well as clothing and posters.

www.jamesondistillery.ie

✚ *Dublin 3c* ✉ Bow Street, Smithfield Village ☎ 01-817 3838 🕐 Daily 10–5:30, guided tours only, every 30 mins
👆 Expensive 🍴 Restaurant and bar (€–€€) 🚌 67, 67a , 68, 69, 79, 90. LUAS to Smithfield

St Patrick's Cathedral
The national cathedral of the protestant Church of Ireland, St Patrick's is arguably the most beautiful religious building in the country. Legend has it that Patrick baptized converts at a well here. The original Early English Gothic-style building was dedicated in 1192. At 93m (305ft), it is the longest church in the country, a fact Oliver Cromwell found useful when he used the nave to stable his cavalry's horses in the 17th century, leaving it in an awful state. The Guinness family paid for much of the original restoration over a hundred years ago. The most famous of St Patrick's deans, the satirical genius Jonathan Swift, has his tomb in the south aisle.

www.stpatrickscathedral.ie

✚ *Dublin 4f* ✉ Patrick's Street, Dublin 2 ☎ 01-453 9472 🕐 Mar–Oct Mon–Sat 9–6, Sun 10–11, 12:45–3, 4:15–6; Nov–Feb Mon–Fri 9–6, Sat 9–5, Sun 10–11, 12:45–3 👆 Moderate 🚌 51b, 78a, 90, 123

Temple Bar

Sooner or later, every visitor to Dublin heads to the area known as Temple Bar, a lively warren of narrow, cobbled streets just south of the Liffey. The word 'bar' means riverside path. There is access from all sides, but the best way in is to walk across the Ha'penny Bridge from the north side of the river and keep straight on through the arch.

You'll find every kind of watering hole and eating place here, from super-touristy pubs like the Oliver St John Gogarty (58–59 Fleet Street; go for the Sunday brunch music session) to bistros and internet cafés. There are interesting galleries, lively pubs, buskers and music just about everywhere.

➕ *Dublin 6d*

Trinity College

Through the Palladian facade of Trinity College is not only an oasis of peace and quiet in the heart of the busy city centre, but also one of Dublin's finest ranges of buildings.

The college was founded in 1592 by Elizabeth I, with many fine buildings from the 18th and 19th centuries. The finest of them all is the **Old Library** (1732), which contains some of Ireland's greatest treasures. Magnificent illuminated manuscripts on display include the 9th-century *Book of Kells* and the *Book of Armagh*.

The main entrance is on College Green, opposite the Bank of Ireland, next to one of the busiest roads in Dublin. On Parliament Square, inside the college grounds, you will find the 19th-century campanile and the elegant 18th-century Dining Hall and the Chapel.

www.tcd.ie

✚ *Dublin 7d*

Old Library

✉ College Green ☎ College: 01-608 2320. Old Library: 01-608 1661 🕒 Old Library: Mon–Sat 9:30–5, Sun 12:30–4:30 (from 9:30 Jun–Sep). Closed 10 days at Christmas ♿ Campus free; Library and *Book of Kells* expensive 🚌 Cross-city buses

More to see in the East

BRÚ NA BÓINNE
Best places to see, ➤ 36–37.

CASTLETOWN HOUSE
Castletown at Celbridge is Ireland's largest and finest Palladian country house, built in the 18th century for William Conolly, Speaker of the Irish House of Commons. The central block, modelled on an Italian *palazzo*, is linked to its two wings with gracefully curving colonnades.

The sumptuous interiors, including the Pompeian Gallery, are largely the inspiration of Lady Louisa Lennox, who came to the house after her marriage in 1758. At its heart is a magnificent hall, with a sweeping cantilevered staircase and superb plasterwork. It's managed by Dúchas, the Irish National Heritage Service. **www.**castletown.ie

🞠 22G ✉ Celbridge ☎ 01-628 8252 🕓 17 Mar to mid-Nov Tue–Sun 10–6 ✋ Inexpensive 🚌 67, 67a from Wellington Quay, Dublin

CEANANNUS MOR (KELLS)

In AD804 a Columban monastery was founded at Kells by monks who had fled the Viking raids on Iona. It was to become one of the great centres of Celtic Christianity, and it was here that the magnificently decorated version of the Gospels, the *Book of Kells*, was completed. This is now a prized possession of Dublin's Trinity College Library (► 88–89), after being moved there during the Cromwellian wars. Replicas are on display in Kells' Heritage Centre, with a multimedia exhibition that entices you to explore the sites throughout Kells.

The town's street pattern reflects the circular shape of the monastery, of which only a round tower and the tiny St Columcille's House remain. The original doorway of the house was 2.4m (8ft) above ground level, a defensive measure which reflected troubled times. Close to the round tower, in the churchyard, are three carved stone crosses, also from the 9th century. A fourth, with 30 decorative panels, stands in Market Square.

🞠 8F ✉ Kells Heritage Centre, The Courthouse, Headfort Place ☎ 046-924 7840 🕓 May–Sep Mon–Sat 10–5:30, Sun and public hols 2–6; Oct–Apr Tue–Sat 10–5 ✋ Inexpensive

GLENDALOUGH

Deep in the heart of the Wicklow Mountains (➤ 102) are
the atmospheric remains of a remarkable monastic city
which was founded in the 6th century by St Kevin and
remained an important place of pilgrimage well into the
18th century.

Many legends surround the mysterious St Kevin. He
is said to have come to Glendalough to avoid worldly
pleasures and the advances of a beautiful redheaded
woman with 'unholy eyes', and that he rolled himself, and
his putative lover, in stinging nettles to dampen their
desire. He may also have hurled the lady into an icy lake
to cool her ardour.

Some of the remains, accessible only by boat, are on the
south side of the Upper Lake and include the reconstructed
Templenaskellig and St Kevin's Bed, a small cave reached after
a difficult climb.

The settlement developed mainly between the 10th and 12th centuries, when most of the buildings were erected. These include St Kevin's Church, an oratory known as St Kevin's Kitchen, the 30m (98ft) round tower and the Cathedral of St Peter and St Paul. There are several other churches and buildings around the site, as well as numerous gravestones and crosses, including the plain granite St Kevin's Cross (3.5m/11ft high). The **Visitor Centre** by the first parking area displays many antiquities found in the valley and is the starting point of guided tours.

✚ 22H

Glendalough Visitor Centre
☎ 040-445325/445352; www.heritageireland.ie ☀ Mid-Mar to mid-Oct daily 9:30–6; mid-Oct to mid-Mar daily 9:30–5 ✋ Inexpensive 🚌 Can be reached on coach tours from Dublin (Bus Éireann)

IRISH NATIONAL HERITAGE PARK

On the River Slaney, a little way west of Wexford, is the Irish National Heritage Park, which recreates Irish life over a period of about 9,000 years, ending with the Anglo-Norman period. No fewer than 14 historical sites have been recreated amid the maturing woodland of the 14ha (34.5-acre) site. The trappings and paraphernalia of everyday life through the ages help to bring it all to

life, and the park successfully combines the requirements of tourism with serious historical content.

✚ 21K ✉ Ferrycarrig ☎ 053-912 0733 ☀ Mar–Oct daily 9:30–6:30; Nov–Feb daily 9:30–5:30 (last admission 3pm) ✋ Moderate 🍴 Restaurant (€€)

JERPOINT ABBEY

Jerpoint Abbey is one of Ireland's finest monastic ruins. The first religious house here was a Benedictine abbey, founded around 1158, but by 1180 it had been taken over by the Cistercians. Substantial remains of buildings from the 12th to the 15th centuries tower above the main road. For all its size and presence, however, what is most interesting here are the amusing carvings along the restored cloister arcade, the fine monuments and various effigies.

✚ 20J ✉ Thomastown ☎ 056-772 4623 🌐 Jun to mid-Sep daily 10–6; mid-Sep to Oct, Mar–May daily 10–5; Nov–Feb daily 10–4 ✋ Inexpensive

KILDARE

This fine old county town has an attractive central square and some medieval buildings. St Brigid's Cathedral is on the site of a monastery founded in AD490 and nearby is a 10th-century round tower with

wonderful views. The other tower in the town is that of the 15th-century castle.

Kildare is at the heart of horse-racing country, and Irish-bred horses are among the most prized in the world. The **National Stud** at Tully House gives visitors an insight into the development and control of these magnificent animals.

The **Japanese Gardens** at Tully House, landscaped between 1906 and 1910 by the Japanese gardener Tasa Eida, include a tea house and a miniature village carved from rock from Mount Fuji. The gardens symbolize the life of man, taking the pilgrim-soul on a journey from Birth to Eternity.

St Fiachra's Garden seeks to recreate the landscape of rocks and water that inspired spirituality in early monastic life. At its heart is a superb bronze statue of St Fiachra, noted for his love of nature, sitting contemplatively, holding up a seed. A stone hermitage contains pieces of sparkling Waterford Crystal representing rocks and flowers.

✚ 21G

National Stud/Japanese Gardens/St Fiachra's Gardens

✉ Tully, Kildare ☎ 045-521617; www.irish-national-stud.ie ⏰ Mid-Feb to mid-Nov daily 9:30–5; mid-Nov to Dec daily 10–5 💷 Moderate
🍽 Restaurant (€€) 🚌 Dublin–Kildare (bus stops at gate)

KILKENNY

Best places to see, ➤ 44–45.

MALAHIDE

The town of Malahide is a traditional seaside resort that has also
become a popular residential area for commuters to Dublin. One
of its great attractions is that it is particularly well endowed with
good restaurants, but its main boast is the magnificent **castle.**
It is one of Ireland's oldest, with a romantic medieval outline

that has changed little in its 800 years. The interior has been transformed over the centuries, and now contains superb Irish furniture and paintings, including a historic portrait collection which is, in effect, a National Portrait Gallery.

www.malahidecastle.com

➕ 10F

Malahide Castle

☎ 01-846 2184 🕓 Apr–Sep Mon–Sat 10–5, Sun and public hols 10–6; Oct–Mar Mon–Sat 10–5, Sun and public hols 11–5 ✋ Moderate 🍴 Restaurant (€€) 🚌 42 from Dublin 🚉 DART Malahide

MONASTERBOICE

One of Ireland's best-known Christian sites, Monasterboice was founded by St Buite in the 6th century and thrived for 600 years, until the new Cistercian Mellifont Abbey superceded it in importance. The site includes a remarkable 10th-century round tower which stands 33m (108ft) high (without its roof) and

offers a good view of the encircling ramparts. There are also three superb high crosses, of which the South Cross (Muiredach's) is the best, a 6m (19.5ft) monolith with distinctive sculptural detail of biblical scenes. The West Cross is the tallest, with some expressive carving, but has suffered from erosion. The North Cross has a plain, modern shaft.

➕ 9E ✉ Collon 🕓 Always accessible 🍴 Forge Gallery Restaurant (€€€), Collon ☎ 041-982 6267

POWERSCOURT HOUSE AND GARDENS

Amid the wild landscape of the Wicklow Mountains
(➤ 102) is one of the most superb gardens in Europe.
Powerscourt Gardens were originally laid out in the
mid-17th century to complement the magnificent
Powerscourt House. Great formal terraces step down
the south-facing slope, with distinctive mosaics of
pebbles (taken from the beach at Bray). There are
beautiful lakes and fountains, statues and decorative
ironwork, American, Italian and Japanese gardens and, in contrast,
charming kitchen gardens and a little pet cemetery. Avid gardeners
who are inspired by all the beauty can visit the Pavilion garden
centre and take a little piece of it home.

In every direction is a backdrop of mountain peaks, and Ireland's
highest waterfall plunges 121m (397ft) into a picturesque valley
within the park. The Glen of the Dargle is a wooded gorge, dotted
with modern sculpture. More than 20 years after it was destroyed
by fire, Powerscourt House reopened its doors. It houses an
exhibition about its history, which includes a visit to the former
ballroom, an excellent gallery of shops and a terrace café.
www.powerscourt.ie

➕ 22G ✉ Enniskerry ☎ 01-204 6000 🕐 Daily 9:30–5:30 (dusk in winter)
🖐 Moderate 🍴 Restaurant (€–€€); kiosk at waterfall 🚌 DART to Bray, then
bus 185 to Enniskerry

WEXFORD

With its huge natural harbour and its location close to the
southeastern point of Ireland, over the centuries Wexford was
the natural landing place for travellers from Wales, Cornwall and
France. The Vikings were the first settlers in the 9th or 10th
century, and the narrow lanes that cluster behind the waterfront
are a legacy of those far-off times. Wexford was also the first Irish
settlement to fall to the invading Anglo-Normans in 1169, and soon
afterwards, at Selskar Abbey, the Anglo-Irish treaty was signed.

Wexford is an interesting mixture of working county town, with busy streets, lively pubs and a famous opera festival, and historic Heritage Town, with some of its 14th-century town wall still intact. The four-storey West Gate houses the Heritage Centre, with an audio-visual presentation about the town.

The nearby mudflats known as The Slobs are now the Wexford Wildfowl Reserve, with a research station, a visitor centre, hides (camouflaged shelters) and a lookout tower. The reserve is of international importance, having one-third of the world's population of Greenland white-fronted geese.

Close by is Johnstown Castle, home of the **Irish Agricultural Museum,** housed in historic farm buildings.

➕ 22K

Irish Agricultural Museum

✉ Johnstown Castle ☎ 053-42888 ⏰ Jun–Aug Mon–Fri 9–5, Sat–Sun and public hols 11–5; Apr–May Mon–Fri 9–12:30, 1:30–5, Sat–Sun 2–5; Sep–Nov Mon–Fri 2–5; Dec–Mar Mon–Fri 9–12:30, 1–5 💰 Moderate 🍴 Coffee shop, Jul–Aug (€)

a drive

around the Wicklow Mountains

This drive includes the beautiful Wicklow Mountains, two of Ireland's finest gardens and the monastic remains at Glendalough.

Leave Wicklow on the Dublin road and continue to Ashford.

Mount Usher Gardens, off to the right along the banks of the River Vartry, are a superb example of 'wild gardens'.

In Ashford turn left, then fork right, following signs for 'Roundwood'. At the T-junction by Roundwood church, turn left, then fork right, signposted 'Enniskerry'. Continue, following signs for Enniskerry.

The entrance to Powerscourt House and Gardens is on a bend at the beginning of the village. The gardens here are among the finest in Europe, and Powerscourt Waterfall is Ireland's highest.

In Enniskerry, turn left, and after 8km (5 miles) reach Glencree. At the next junction head for 'Sally

Gap, Glendalough'. After another 8km (5 miles) turn right, and keep following signs for 'Blessington' until you reach the N81. Turn left. After 3km (2 miles) turn left onto the R758 signposted 'Valleymount, Lake Drive'. Continue, following signs for Glendalough.

This interesting ancient settlement is one of Ireland's major attractions, with atmospheric ruins.

Return to the junction and go on through Laragh. After 5km (3 miles) turn right, signposted 'Arklow, Rathdrum R755'. In Rathdrum follow signs for 'Avoca'. At the T-junction, turn left, then bear right, signposted 'Dublin'. After 13km (8 miles) turn right to return to Wicklow.

Distance 117km (73 miles)
Time About 5–6 hours, depending on attractions visited
Start/end point Wicklow ✚ 23H
Lunch Powerscourt Terrace Café (€)
✉ Powerscourt House
☎ 01-204 6070

THE WICKLOW MOUNTAINS

Just a short distance from the centre of Dublin (▶ 82–89) is this wonderfully secluded area of high mountains and peaceful valleys. Lugnaquilla is the highest point, at 925m (3,035ft), and is the source of the River Slaney. Two scenic passes cross the mountains from east to west – the Sally Gap on the old Military Road and the Wicklow Gap further south.

Great forests clothe many of the mountain slopes, including Coollatin Park near Shillelagh, in the south, which preserves remnants of the oak forests which are said to have supplied the roof timbers for Dublin's St Patrick's Cathedral and London's Palace of Westminster. Near Blessington is the great Pollaphuca Reservoir, providing Dublin with both water and electricity, with scenic lakeside drives and waterbus cruises.

Signs of historic habitation include ancient hillforts and stone circles, the monastic site at Glendalough (▶ 92–93) and the mansions of Powerscourt at Eniskerry (▶ 98) and Russborough House, near Blessington. More sinister associations are attached to the creepy ruin of the Hell Fire Club on top of Mount Pelier near Tallaght. Ask the locals to tell you its story, then climb up (in daylight!) for a look. The views are wonderful.

✚ 22H ⅋ Johnnie Fox's, Glencullen (€€) ☎ 01-295 5647

HOTELS

AVOCA, CO WICKLOW
Sheepwalk House (€)
A cosy 18th-century house 3km (2 miles) from Avoca, with lovely views over the Arklow Valley.

✉ Beech Road, Avoca ☎ 0402-35189; www.sheepwalk.com 🕔 Closed Dec–Jan

DUBLIN, CO DUBLIN
Charleville Lodge (€–€€)
This highly recommended guest house is in a Victorian terrace near Phoenix Park.

✉ 268–272 North Circular Road ☎ 01-838 6633; www.charlevillelodge.ie
🕔 Closed 21–26 Dec

Kilronan House (€€)
Stylish Georgian house in a peaceful location close to the National Concert Hall.

✉ 70 Adelaide Road ☎ 01-475 5266; www.dublinn.com

Merrion (€€€)
The epitome of relaxed grandeur, the Merrion, comprising four gracious Georgian town houses, has superb bedrooms and opulent bathrooms that reflect the 18th-century architecture.

✉ Upper Merrion Street ☎ 01-603 0600; www.merrionhotel.com

Number 31 (€€–€€€)
These two Georgian mews have been decorated in contrasting modern and period styles to make the perfect Dublin guest house, not far from Stephen's Green.

✉ 31 Leeson Close ☎ 01-676 2929; www.number31.ie

Park Inn (€€)
In revitalized Smithfield Village, this luxurious hotel has hyper-modern designs and a delightful rooftop garden.

✉ Smithfield Village ☎ 01-817 3838; www.dublinparkinn.ie

KILKENNY, CO KILKENNY
Butler House (€€–€€€)
Georgian mansion with elegant interiors, restored by the Irish State Design Agency. Peaceful location, but close enough to the city centre and castle to be a good base for sightseeing.

✉ 16 Patrick Street ☎ 056-776 5707; www.butler.ie ⏰ Closed 24–29 Dec

RATHNEW, CO WICKLOW
Hunters Hotel (€€€)
Rambling 16th-century coaching inn has loads of character and lovely gardens running down to the river. Good restaurant featuring some excellent fish dishes.

✉ Newrath Bridge ☎ 0404-40106; www.hunters.ie

Tinakilly Country House (€€–€€€)
This elegant mansion is set in 3ha (7.5 acres), with sea views.

☎ 0404-69274; www.tinakilly.ie

STRAFFAN, CO KILDARE
Kildare Hotel and Country Club (€€€)
Sheer luxury and excellent food in magnificent surroundings. Facilities include a golf course and private fishing.

☎ 01-601 7200; www.kclub.ie

RESTAURANTS

DALKEY, CO DUBLIN
Guinea Pig (The Fish Restaurant) (€€€)
Family-run restaurant, adorned with rustic brass ornaments and decorative plates, with an extensive, though not exclusively, seafood-based menu.

✉ 17 Railway Road, Dalkey ☎ 01-285 9055 ⏰ Dinner only

DUBLIN, CO DUBLIN
Café Mao (€€)
Fashionable eatery with a slick interior, serving delicious stir fries and oriental dishes such as Malaysian chicken.

✉ 2–3 Chatham Row ☎ 01-670 4899 ⏰ Lunch, dinner

Chapter One (€€€)

A classy gem on the Northside, this French-inspired restaurant is located in the basement of the Dublin Writers Museum.

✉ 18–19 Parnell Square ☎ 01-873 2266 🕐 Lunch, dinner Tue–Sat

Elephant and Castle (€)

Buzzy, youthful café-restaurant that was one of Temple Bar's first new-wave places and is still one of the best. Good, generous salads, pasta dishes and home-made burgers. Friendly, but rather slow service.

✉ 18 Temple Bar ☎ 01-679 3121 🕐 Lunch, dinner

Il Baccaro (€€)

Intimate Italian restaurant set in a lovely 17th-century cellar in the heart of Temple Bar.

✉ Diceman's Corner ☎ 01-671 4597 🕐 Lunch (Fri–Sun), dinner

Patrick Guilbaud (€€€)

See page 59.

Queen of Tarts (€)

Super home-made cakes and pastries. Salads and cream teas, too. All served in intimate surroundings by friendly staff.

✉ 4 Cork Hill, Dame Street ☎ 01-670 7499 🕐 Daily

Thai Orchid (€€)

Delicious Thai food and courteous service from Thai staff in traditional costume.

✉ 7 Westmoreland Street ☎ 01-671 9969 🕐 Lunch Mon–Fri; dinner daily

ENNISKERRY, CO WICKLOW
Powerscourt Terrace Café (€)

Wonderful views over the Powerscourt gardens and to the mountains beyond.

✉ Powerscourt House ☎ 01-204 6070 🕐 Lunch only

GLENCULLEN, CO DUBLIN
Johnnie Fox's Pub (€€)
An 18th-century coaching inn, complete with beams and open
fires, known for its excellent seafood, with fresh mussels a
speciality. Music and dancing nightly.
✉ Dublin Mountains ☎ 01-295 5647 ⏱ Lunch, dinner; closed Sun lunch,
Good Fri and 25 Dec

GREYSTONES, CO WICKLOW
Hungry Monk (€€€)
The place for a romantic candlelit supper overlooking a scenic golf
course. Good traditional Irish dishes.
✉ Church Road ☎ 01-287 5759 ⏱ Dinner Wed–Sat, lunch Sun only

HOWTH, CO DUBLIN
King Sitric Fish Restaurant (€€€)
Co Dublin's best-known fish restaurant.
✉ East Pier ☎ 01-832 5235 ⏱ Lunch Mon–Fri, dinner Mon–Sat; closed Sun

KILDARE, CO KILDARE
Chapter 16 (€€)
Modern, bright new addition to the local dining scene, with a solid
menu touched with moments of imagination.
✉ The Square ☎ 045-522232 ⏱ Lunch, dinner

KILKENNY, CO KILKENNY
Kilkenny Design Centre (€)
The restaurant at this complex of craft workshops matches up to
the quality Irish craft wares on sale. Traditional Irish dishes and
vegetarian selections.
✉ Castle Yard ☎ 056-772 2118 ⏱ Daily during shopping hours

KILMACANOGE, CO WICKLOW
Avoca Handweavers (€)
Set in the Wicklow Mountains and serving delicious home-cooked
food. Good selection for vegetarians.
✉ Kilmacanoge ☎ 01-286 7466 ⏱ Mon–Sat 9:30–5:30, Sun 10–6

LEIGHLINBRIDGE, CO CARLOW
The Lord Bagenal Inn (€€)
Country pub serving international and Irish cuisine.

✉ Main Street ☎ 059-972 1668 🕐 Lunch, dinner 12–6. Bar meals Mon–Sat 9am–10pm, Sun 9–9

MALAHIDE, CO DUBLIN
Bon Appetit (€€€)
There is a first-class wine list to accompany the international menu with seafood specialities.

✉ 9 James Terrace ☎ 01-845 0314 🕐 Lunch, dinner; closed Sun and public hols, Sat lunch

ROUNDWOOD, CO WICKLOW
Roundwood Inn (€€)
Cosy pub offering seafood, game and traditional Irish dishes.

✉ Roundwood ☎ 01-281 8107 🕐 Restaurant: lunch Sun only, dinner Fri–Sun. Pub food daily, all day

WEXFORD, CO WEXFORD
The Wrens Nest (€)
A great place to meet the locals. Good bar meals.

✉ Custom House Quay ☎ 053-22359 🕐 Lunch Mon–Sat until 3pm

SHOPPING

CRAFTS
Avoca Handweavers
The oldest working woollen mill in Ireland. All kinds of Irish-made crafts. Tea room.

✉ Avoca, Co Wicklow ☎ 01-286 7466 🕐 Daily 9:30–5:30

Bogwood Sculpture Studio
Beautiful sculptures; video and photographs tell the story of the 5,000-year-old bogwood.

✉ Barley Harbour, Newtowncashel, Co Longford ☎ 043-25297
🕐 Mon–Sat 9–6

Cleo
Clothes made from natural fibres of Irish origin.
✉ 18 Kildare Street, Dublin, Co Dublin ☎ 01-676 1421 ⏰ Mon–Sat 9–5:30

Design Yard
Features some of the best contemporary Irish craftworkers.
✉ 48–49 Nassau Street, Dublin, Co Dublin ☎ 01-474 1011 ⏰ Daily 10–5:30

Kilkenny Design Centre
Made in Ireland is the key here. Large selection of pottery, jewellery, glassware and fashion items. Traditional but with a touch of new creativity.
✉ 6–10 Nassau Street, Dublin, Co Dublin ☎ 01-677 7066 ⏰ Mon–Sat 8:30–7, Sun 11–6

Kilkenny Design Centre
Superb range of top-quality crafts from all over Ireland.
✉ Castle Yard, Kilkenny, Co Kilkenny ☎ 056-772 2118 ⏰ Mon–Sat 10–7, Sun 11–7. Closed Jan–early Apr

TRADITIONAL MUSIC
Celtic Note
Small, specialist Irish music store featuring everything from folk and traditional ballads to rock and contemporary.
✉ 12 Nassau Street, Dublin, Co Dublin ☎ 01-670 4157

Claddagh Records
A treasure trove of CDs and tapes ranging from Irish dance to traditional and modern.
✉ Cecelia Street, Temple Bar, Dublin, Co Dublin ☎ 01-677 0262

DEPARTMENT STORES
There are large malls at Blackrock (a short walk from DART Blackrock station), Blanchardstown (north on the N3) and the Liffey Valley Centre (west off the N4, just beyond the M50 interchange).

The Square Towncentre at Tallaght, south of Dublin, is a superb modern shopping centre, the largest in Ireland, with nearly 150 shops under a huge dome of natural light. Trees and shrubs thrive here, creating an illusion of the outdoors, where it never rains. The centre, open daily, includes a multiscreen cinema, restaurants, a free crèche (day nursery) and free parking for 3,000 cars.

Arnotts
A major refurbishment has put this store at the forefront of the new-look Northside.
✉ 12 Henry Street, Dublin, Co Dublin ☎ 01-805 0400 ◐ Mon–Sat 9–6:30 (to 9:30pm Thu), Sun 12–6

Brown Thomas
Sophisticated store, with top-quality goods, including designer fashions, cosmetics and china. Cafés and a hair salon.
✉ 88–92 Grafton Street, Dublin, Co Dublin ☎ 01-605 6666 ◐ Mon–Sat 9–8 (to 9pm Thu), Sun 10–7

Clery's
Ireland's only remaining Irish-owned department store; as well as all the usual things, it is good for souvenirs.
✉ O'Connell Street, Dublin, Co Dublin ☎ 01-878 6000 ◐ Mon–Sat 9–6:30 (to 9pm Thu, 8pm Fri), Sun 12–6

ENTERTAINMENT

LIVE MUSIC
The Button Factory
A music venue that also hosts club nights, live music, dances and fashion shows.
✉ Curved Street, Dublin, Co Dublin ☎ 01-670 9202

Johnnie Fox's
Music every day.
✉ Glencullen, Co Dublin ☎ 01-295 5647

O'Shea's Merchant
Traditional music and dancing. You'll be encouraged to dance.
✉ 12 Lower Bridge Street, Dublin, Co Dublin ☎ 01-679 6793

The Point
This vast venue in a former tram depot attracts music and dance superstars.

✉ East Link Bridge, North Wall Quay, Dublin, Co Dublin ☎ 01-836 6777

Whelans
Famous Dublin music venue, hosting traditional Irish, rock, jazz and blues.

✉ 25 Wexford Street, Dublin, Co Dublin ☎ 01-478 0766

NIGHTCLUBS
Lillie's Bordello
✉ Adam Court, Grafton Street, Dublin, Co Dublin ☎ 01-679 9204

POD
✉ 35 Harcourt Street, Dublin, Co Dublin ☎ 01-478 0225

The Village
✉ 26 Wexford Street, Dublin, Co Dublin ☎ 01-475 8555

THEATRE AND CINEMA
Abbey Theatre
✉ 26 Abbey Street, Dublin, Co Dublin ☎ 01-878 7222

Gaiety Theatre
✉ South King Street, Dublin, Co Dublin ☎ 01-677 1717

Gate Theatre
✉ 1 Cavendish Row, Parnell Square, Dublin, Co Dublin ☎ 01-874 4045

Irish Film Institute
✉ 6 Eustace Street, Temple Bar, Dublin, Co Dublin ☎ 01-679 5744

The South

A great many visitors to Ireland head straight for this southwestern corner, with its quintessentially Irish look and feel. Here you will find the great fiord-like bays which cut into the rocky west coast, between the magnificent peninsulas of An Daingean (The Dingle), the Iveragh (better known as The Ring of Kerry), the Beara and the smaller, but no less beautiful Sheep's Head and Mizen peninsulas.

Cork

The south coast is less spectacular, but has some wonderful beaches, fine resorts and charming fishing villages such as Kinsale. Aim to be hungry when you visit here – the village is known as the Gourmet Capital of Ireland.

The southwest is not all coast and scenery. Ireland's second city, Cork, and its third, Limerick, are in this area, while towards the east are the historic city of Waterford, the great Rock of Cashel and the ancient towns and castles along the River Suir.

CORK

Cork is the Republic's second largest city. At its heart is the wide St Patrick's Street, with lots of lanes leading off that are a delight to explore. Cork is a friendly city, where tradition and modern life blend together easily. It has a vibrant arts and cultural scene and was designated the European Capital of Culture for 2005.

The name Cork comes from the Irish word 'Corcaigh', meaning marsh. The older part of the city is on an island in the River Lee. From this island a network of streets branches out, giving a blend of broad malls and narrow lanes, spires, Georgian houses, busy

markets and bridges that make up Cork's most prevalent features. The Lee flows into the deep waters of Cork Harbour, and this harbour brought much of the city's prosperity over the centuries. It also brought the Vikings in AD820 and later the Anglo-Normans. Cork suffered at the hands of William of Orange in 1690 and the 'Black and Tans' (a British military force) in the 20th century. Having risen to all these challenges, Cork remains a city of unique character.

✠ 18L

ℹ Grand Parade ☎ 021-425 5100

Cork Butter Museum

Butter seems an odd subject for a museum, until you discover that Shandon's Butter Exchange was the largest butter market in the world, attracting customers from distant continents, and that its brand was internationally recognized as a symbol of top quality.

www.corkbutter.museum

✉ O'Connell Square, Shandon ☎ 021-430 0600 🕔 Mar–Oct daily 10–1, 2–5 (Jul–Aug 2–6) 💷 Inexpensive 🚌 3 from city centre

Cork City Gaol

The thought of going to prison, if only for the afternoon, may not appeal, but Cork's former gaol is now a museum that recreates prison life in the 19th century in an entertaining way, and also presents a good social history of the city. The former Governor's House contains the Radio Museum Experience, incorporating a 1927 studio and the RTE Museum Collection.

www.corkcitygaol.com

✉ Sunday's Well ☎ 021-430 5022 🕔 Mar–Oct daily 9:30–5; Nov–Feb daily 10–4 💷 Moderate 🍴 Coffee shop (€)

Cork Public Museum

Few city museums have such a lovely setting as this. There are 7.5ha (18.5 acres) of beautiful parkland surrounding the Georgian House, which displays a wide range of collections illustrating the economic and social history of Cork, along with its Civic Regalia.

✉ Fitzgerald Park, Mardyke ☎ 021-427 0679 ⏰ Mon–Fri 11–1, 2:15–5 (until 6pm Jan–Aug), Sat 11–1, 2:15–4, Sun 3–5 (Apr–Sep). Closed Sun and public hols ✋ Free

Crawford Art Gallery

One of Ireland's finest art galleries, the Crawford has a wonderful extension. Above a glass frontage on Half Moon Street, the gallery wall swoops out over the pavement like the hull of a ship, to reflect Cork's maritime heritage. The theme continues inside, in the three curving ceiling sections above the upper galleries, that are flooded with natural light. The lower gallery has a more restrained environment. The next phase of the Crawford Development Plan is to improve the historic original building and the grounds. As well as its permanent collection of works by Irish artists, there are lively temporary exhibitions.

www.crawfordartgallery.com

✉ Emmet Place ☎ 021-427 3377 ⏰ Mon–Sat 10–5. Closed 25 Dec–1 Jan, Sun and public hols ✋ Free 🍴 Crawford Gallery Restaurant (€€) 🚌 All city buses 🚂 Cork (10-min walk)

St Anne's Church

The tall square tower of St Anne's Church, capped by a gilded weathervane in the shape of a salmon, is Cork's best-known landmark. The tower is faced in red and white sandstone – the colours of Cork. Built in 1722, St Anne's is the oldest parish church still in continuous use in Cork. Its famous bells chime each quarter hour. Sunday service is at 10am.

✉ Church Street, Shandon ☎ 021-450 5906 ⏰ Apr–Sep daily 9–6; Oct–Mar daily 10–4 ✋ Inexpensive 🚌 3 from city centre

a walk around Cork

This walk takes in the main shopping street and the art gallery, before crossing the River Lee to Shandon, then on to the Cork Public Museum in Fitzgerald Park.

Walk along Grand Parade away from the statue, then bear right into St Patrick Street. At the pedestrian crossing, turn left and go along Academy Street to the Crawford Art Gallery (➤ 114).

This fine municipal gallery has a particularly good collection of local landscapes.

Continue around the corner and cross the bridge. Turn left, then bear right and follow signs to Shandon for the Butter Museum (➤ 113). Off the square is St Anne's Church (➤ 114).

This Anglican Communion church is one of Cork's landmarks, with its lofty tower and famous bells.

Continue, passing the Shandon Arms on the left, and at the end go straight along Chapel Street.

Opposite the end of Chapel Street is the Cathedral of St Mary and St Ann, with a beautiful, bright interior and some interesting monuments.

Turn left along Cathedral Street, then left down Shandon Street to the river. Turn right to walk along the nearside riverbank, then at the end cross a footbridge. Follow the riverside wall then go forward between Mercy Hospital and Lee Maltings. At the end turn right and walk along Dyke Parade until you reach the gates to Fitzgerald Park on the right. The Cork Public Museum is just inside the gates (➤ 114).

Distance About 2.5km (1.5 miles)
Time About 3 hours
Start point Grand Parade 🚌 All city centre buses
End point Fitzgerald Park 🚌 8 to city centre
Lunch Bells Bar and Bistro (€–€€) ✉ Quality Shandon Court Hotel, Shandon ☎ 021-455 1793

More to see in the South

BANTRY

This lovely little town, at the head of the beautiful Bantry Bay, is a busy fishing port, its harbour overlooked by a statue of that intrepid Irish seafarer, St Brendan. Close by is the entrance to **Bantry House,** an exquisite Georgian mansion. The elegant interior contains a fine collection of furniture, Pompeiian mosaics and tapestries. The Italianate gardens have a wonderful view over the bay and delicate plants thrive in the mild climate.

www.bantryhouse.ie

✚ 16M

Bantry House

☎ 027-50047 ⊙ Mar–Oct daily 9–6 🎫 Expensive 🍴 Coffee shop (€)
🚌 Cork–Bantry bus

THE BEARA PENINSULA

Less well known than the Ring of Kerry and The Dingle, The Beara

Peninsula is just as beautiful, with its rocky, indented coastline and offshore islands. The Caha Mountains and the Slieve Miskish Mountains form its spine, creating a dramatic inland landscape, and the Healy Pass, which zigzags across the Caha range, has wonderful views (► 124).

The **Sub-Tropical Gardens** on Garinish Island, in a sheltered inlet of Bantry Bay, reached by ferry from Glengarriff, is the Beara's main attraction. It is a magnificent

Italian garden, with a world-famous collection of plants, which thrive here because of the warming effect of the Gulf Stream.

➕ 15L

Sub-Tropical Gardens

✉ Garinish Island, off Glengarriff ☎ 027-63040; www.heritageireland.ie

🕐 Jul–Aug Mon–Sat 9:30–6:30, Sun 11–6:30; Apr–Jun, Sep Mon–Sat 10–6:30, Sun 11–6:30; Mar, Oct Mon–Sat 10–4:30, Sun 1–5 ✋ Inexpensive

🚌 Glengarriff main street; Kenmare–Bantry bus passes through Glengarriff

🚢 Glengarriff main street (separate charge for ferry)

BLARNEY CASTLE

The 'gift of the Blarney' is known all over the world and this is where you get it. By leaning backwards over a sheer drop (protected by railings) from the castle battlements and kissing a particular piece of rock, any visitor can go home endowed with a new eloquence. The Blarney Stone is reached by ancient stone spiral staircases through the ruins of the 15th-century castle, which would be well worth a visit even without its notoriety. The castle is set amid lovely grounds, and is one of Ireland's most visited places.

www.blarneycastle.ie

➕ 17L ✉ Blarney, Co Cork ☎ 021-438 5210 🕐 Jun–Aug daily 9–7; May, Sep daily 9–6:30; daily 9–dusk rest of year ✋ Moderate

CASHEL

The town tends to be overshadowed by the great Rock of Cashel (▶ 52–53) which dominates the skyline, but as one of Ireland's Heritage Towns, it is well worth a visit in its own right. A good place to start is City Hall, which has historical and folklore displays relating to the town. There is also a **Folk Village,** with a series of 18th- to 20th-century house fronts, shops and memorabilia, and the **Brù Borù Heritage Centre,** which offers a cultural experience through its folk theatre, evening banquets, exhibitions and traditional music sessions. Added in 2001, 'The Sounds of

History' exhibition is located in a subterranean setting where Ireland's musical heritage is reactivated and enhanced.

www.cashel.ie

✚ 19J 🚍 Dublin–Cork buses 🚆 Thurles 18km (11 miles)

Folk Village

✉ Dominic Street ☎ 062-62525 🕐 Daily 9:30–7:30 (until 6pm in winter) ✋ Moderate

Brù Borù Heritage Centre

☎ 062-61122 🕐 Mid-Jun to mid-Sep daily 9am–11pm, shows Tue–Sat 9pm; mid-Sep to mid-Jun, Mon–Fri 9–1, 2–5, no shows ✋ Exhibition moderate; show expensive 🍴 Self-service restaurant (€). Combined evening meal and show (€€)

CORCA DHUIBHNE (THE DINGLE PENINSULA)

Best places to see, ➤ 40–41.

KENMARE

Kenmare's location at the head of Kenmare Bay, surrounded by majestic mountains, earns the town its Irish name 'Neidin' or 'little nest'. Ireland's first planned town was designed by William Petty in 1670. Today, traditional pubs, craft shops and art galleries combine well with first-class hotels, guest houses and award-winning restaurants. The Heritage Centre explains the history of Kenmare using personal audio-tours and exhibitions include exhibits on Kenmare lace and the Nun of Kenmare.

✚ 15L 🍴 P F McCarthy's, Main Street (€€)
ℹ️ Tourist Information ☎ 064-41233

THE RING OF KERRY

The road which encircles the Iveragh peninsula is popularly known as the Ring of Kerry, an exceptionally scenic circular

route of 107km (66 miles) if you start and finish in Killarney. From here you go south through the national park to Kenmare, then strike out along the north shore of the Kenmare estuary, through the lovely resort of Parknasilla. The famous Great Southern Hotel here has played host to the rich and famous for many years.

Farther along is Caherdaniel. The route heads north from here around Ballinskelligs Bay to Waterville, then on to Cahersiveen, the 'capital' of the peninsula and birthplace of the politician Daniel O'Connell. It also has an interesting Heritage Centre. The road then heads eastwards, with Dingle Bay to the north, through Killorglin, a market town famous for its Puck Fair in August, then back to Killarney.

As if the wonderful coast and mountain scenery were not enough, the peninsula is also blessed with a warm Gulf Stream climate.

✚ 14L 🍴 Blind Piper Bar Restaurant (€–€€), Caherdaniel
ℹ️ Killarny Tourist Information ☎ 064-31633

KILLARNEY

Killarney is one of the busiest tourist towns in Ireland, not for its own attractions so much as for its surroundings.

Although it has many pubs and shops, it is essentially a base for exploring the beauties of Kerry, and is the traditional starting point for the Ring of Kerry. The Killarney National Park, 10,000ha (24,710 acres) of beautiful mountains, woodland and lakes, is right on the doorstep, and is the setting for Muckross House (➤ 46–47).

Jarveys are the drivers of the horse-drawn jaunting cars you will see lined up along the roadside in Killarney. Haggling over the fee is an acceptable part of the deal, but remember that you are not just paying to get from A to B – jarveys are an intrinsic part of the Killarney experience and will usually spin a yarn or two along the way.

✛ 15K

around Kerry and Cork

This drive includes the wonderful wooded mountains of the Killarney National Park, the spectacular Healy Pass and two of Ireland's finest historic houses.

From Killarney take the N71, signposted to Muckross, and soon you will reach the Killarney National Park and Muckross House (▶ 46–47).

Muckross's location amid the mountains and lakes of the national park is unsurpassed.

Continue on the N71, passing Torc Waterfall, to reach Ladies' View, then after 6km (4 miles), at Molls Gap, bear left, signposted to Kenmare, Glengarriff. At Kenmare drive up the main street and turn right, then leave the town following signs for Glengarriff and Bantry. Cross a river bridge and turn right, signposted Castletown Bearhaven R571. Continue for about 14km (8.5 miles), then follow signs for the Healy Pass.

This pass across the Caha Mountains has stunning views and a breathtaking summit.

Over the top of the pass, descend a series of hairpin bends and continue to reach a T-junction. Turn left for Glengarriff or right to lunch in Castletownbere.

Garinish Island, with its beautiful Sub-Tropical Gardens, can be reached by ferry from Glengarriff.

Continue for 5.6km (3.5 miles) to Bantry.

By the harbour on the Cork road is Bantry House (➤ 118) and the Armada Exhibition.

Retrace the route to Glengarriff, then take the N71 to Kenmare and Killarney.

Distance 140km (87 miles)
Time 6–7 hours depending on attractions visited
Start/end point Killarney ✚ 15K
Lunch The Copper Kettle (€) ✉ The Square, Castletownbere
☎ 027-71792 ◑ Mon–Sat

KINSALE

Kinsale is a delightful little town 29km (18 miles) from Cork City. It offers visitors such things as sailing, scenery, history and good food. The annual Gourmet Festival in October and a Good Food Circle work to maintain the town's famously high culinary standards. Historically, Kinsale is remembered for the 1601 battle when a Spanish fleet came to aid Hugh O'Neill's struggle against the English. The Irish/Spanish force was defeated, thus marking the decline of the old Gaelic order, with the 'Flight of the Earls' to Europe. The late 17th-century Charles Fort at Summercove is open to visitors, while James Fort is in ruins but is still worth a visit for the grand views of the town and harbour. It was off this coast that the *Lusitania* was sunk by a German submarine in 1915, with the loss of 1,500 lives. Places of interest to visit in Kinsale include the Courthouse, *c*1600, which now houses a regional museum

✚ 17M 🍴 Fishy Fishy (€€), Guardwell ☎ 021-477 4453
ℹ Tourist Information ☎ 021-477 2234

LIMERICK

The Republic's third largest city, Limerick is a cultural centre, well endowed with theatres, art galleries and museums – notably the **Hunt Museum.** Located in the elegant 18th-century Custom House, the gallery has one of the greatest private collections of art and antiquities in the country.

The River Shannon flows through the city, overlooked by **King John's Castle** and crossed by many fine bridges. The oldest part of the city is on King's Island, first settled by the Vikings, and it is here that the most important historical sites are found, including the castle and the 12th-century Protestant cathedral.

The city's architecture is jealously guarded by the Limerick Civic Trust. The best old street is The Crescent, while examples of modern architecture are the Civic Centre and City Hall on Merchant's Quay.

✚ 17J

Hunt Museum

✉ Custom House, Rutland Street ☎ 061-312833; www.huntmuseum.com
🕐 Mon–Sat 10–5, Sun 2–5 🍴 Restaurant (€€) 🖐 Moderate
🚌 All city centre buses

King John's Castle

✚ Nicholas Street, King's Island ☎ 061-360788 🕐 Apr–Oct daily 10–5:30; Nov–Mar daily 10:30–4:30 🖐 Moderate

MUCKROSS HOUSE

Best places to see, ➤ 46–47.

ROCK OF CASHEL

Best places to see, ➤ 52–53.

WATERFORD

Waterford grew from an ancient Viking settlement into the foremost port in Ireland, and its quays are still busy with international trade; the famous **Waterford Crystal Visitor Centre** reflects this. The city preserves an atmosphere of the past, and the mixture of Celt, Viking, Norman, English, Huguenot and Flemish gives a European flavour which is reflected on the seafront and in its narrow lanes. One of the oldest buildings is Reginald's Tower, built by the Vikings in 1003, which now houses the city museum. The Church of Ireland cathedral is regarded as the finest 18th-century ecclesiastical building in Ireland, and the Catholic cathedral has superb carving and stained glass.

www.waterfordvisitorcentre.com

➕ 20K

Waterford Crystal Visitor Centre

✉ Kilbarry ☎ 051-332500 🕓 Visitor centre and shop: Mar–Oct daily 9–6; Nov–Feb daily 9–5. Tours: Mar–Oct daily 9–4:15; Nov–Feb Mon–Fri 9–3:15
✋ Moderate 🍴 Restaurant (€–€€) 🚌 Waterford–Ballybeg

HOTELS

ADARE, CO LIMERICK

Adare Manor (€€€)

An opulent hotel in a Gothic mansion, surrounded by parkland beside the River Maigue. Includes a championship golf course and other leisure facilities.

✉ On Limerick to Tralee route ☎ 061-396566; www.adaremanor.com

CLONAKILTY, CO CORK

Inchydoney Island Lodge & Spa (€€€)

Modern coastal hotel in blue flag beach setting. Home to Ireland's only thalassotherapy (seawater) spa.

✉ Clonakilty, West Cork ☎ 023-33143; www.inchydoneyisland.com

CORK, CO CORK

Hotel Isaacs (€€)

One of Cork's finest hotels, with good accommodation and the celebrated Greenes Restaurant.

✉ 48 MacCurtain Street ☎ 021-450 3805; www.isaacs.ie

KENMARE, CO KERRY

Park Hotel (€€€)

Country-house hotel overlooking Kenmare Bay and home to the deluxe spa 'Samas'.

✉ On the R569 ☎ 064-41200; www.parkkenmare.com ④ Closed 4 Jan to 10 Apr

Sallyport House (€€)

This 1932, antique-filled family home has been enlarged into a delightful bed-and-breakfast, with lovely grounds including an orchard.

✉ Glengariff Road ☎ 064-42066; www.sallyporthouse.com

KILLARNEY, CO KERRY

Aghadoe Heights (€€€)

In a superb setting high above the Killarney Lakes, this hotel offers luxury and hospitality and an excellent restaurant.

✉ 5km (3 miles) north of Killarney, off the N22 Tralee road ☎ 064-31766; www.aghadoeheights.com 🕐 Closed Jan–Mar

KINSALE, CO CORK
Deasy's Long Quay House (€€)
Splendid Georgian residence overlooking the inner harbour and yacht marina.
✉ Long Quay ☎ 021-477 4563; www.longquayhousekinsale.com 🕐 Closed Nov, Dec

LIMERICK, CO LIMERICK
Best Western Pery's Hotel (€€)
This historic city-centre hotel is in the heart of Georgian Limerick, and is perfect for shopping and restaurants.
✉ Glentworth Street ☎ 061-413822; www.perys.ie

WATERFORD, CO WATERFORD
Waterford Castle & Golf Club (€€€)
A real castle on an island with many of its original features, including 16th-century oak panelling, stone walls and graceful arches, and modern leisure facilities including adjacent 18-hole, par 72 championship golf course.
✉ The Island, Ballinakill ☎ 051-878203; www.waterfordcastle.com

RESTAURANTS

BALLINGARRY, CO LIMERICK
The Mustard Seed (€€€€)
A pleasant drive through the Limerick countryside on quiet lanes leads to this first-class restaurant in a stylish country house. Also offers B&B.
✉ Echo Lodge ☎ 069-68508 🕐 Dinner only; closed 24–26 Dec

BALTIMORE, CO CORK
Chez Youen (€€–€€€)
Among the best fish restaurants in Ireland.
✉ The Square ☎ 028-20136 🕐 Lunch Sun only, dinner daily in summer, Thu–Sat in winter

BANTRY, CO CORK
O'Connor's Seafood Restaurant (€–€€)
Fresh local fish and shellfish are the specialities here.
✉ The Square ☎ 027-50221 🕓 Lunch, dinner

CLOGHROE, CO CORK
Blairs Inn (€–€€)
In a secluded riverside setting near Blarney. Good Irish cuisine, including fish, duck, steaks and game, all from local sources. Traditional music on Mondays (summer only).
✉ Cloghroe, Blarney ☎ 021-438 1470 🕓 Lunch, dinner, all-day bar menu

CORK, CO CORK
Farmgate Café (€–€€)
An informal but delicious and atmospheric lunch spot in the covered English Market in Princes Street. A real gem.
✉ English Market ☎ 021-427 8134 🕓 Lunch Mon–Sat

Jacques (€€)
Well-reviewed restaurant creating modern Irish dishes from excellent local produce, including farm-reared ducks, fish and organic vegetables.
✉ Phoenix Street ☎ 021-427 7387 🕓 Lunch, dinner Mon–Sat

DINGLE, CO KERRY
The Charterhouse Restaurant (€€)
Excellent cuisine in this cosy harbourside restaurant.
✉ The Mail Raod ☎ 066-915 2255 🕓 Dinner daily Mar–Oct; Nov–Feb Thu–Sun; closed 6 Jan–13 Feb

Lord Baker's (€–€€)
Fish, game and succulent steaks are the speciality of this excellent restaurant.
✉ Main Street ☎ 066-915 1277 🕓 Lunch, dinner; closed Thu and 24–26 Dec

KENMARE, CO KERRY
Packie's (€€)
Stylish but unpretentious restaurant with creative cooking; intensely flavoured Irish-Mediterranean food.

✉ Henry Street ☎ 064-41508 🕐 Dinner Mon–Sat; closed mid-Jan to Feb

Prego (€–€€)
Good atmosphere and tasty food in this well-priced family restaurant.

✉ Henry Street ☎ 064-42350 🕐 Lunch, dinner

KILLARNEY, CO KERRY
Foley's Seafood and Steak Restaurant (€€–€€€)
The name says it all, and the restaurant is famous for it.

✉ 23 High Street ☎ 064-31217 🕐 Lunch, dinner; closed 24–26 Dec and lunch in winter

Panis Angelicus (€)
This stylish, contemporary café is famous locally for its home-made Irish potato cake with garlic. Live jazz adds to the chilled-out feeling.

✉ 15 New Street ☎ 064-39648 🕐 No dinner Oct–Apr

KINSALE, CO CORK
Fishy Fishy (€€)
Fresh fish, shellfish, salads and desserts feature in this popular seafood speciality eatery.

✉ Market Place ☎ 021-477 4453 🕐 Daily 10–4

Man Friday (€€–€€€)
One of Kinsale's longest-established restaurants, with an excellent reputation for its modern Irish and international cuisine.

✉ Scilly ☎ 021-477 2260 🕐 Dinner only; closed Sun (except public hols)

LIMERICK, CO LIMERICK
Freddy's Bistro (€€)
This restaurant, serving Irish and continental dishes, is full of character.

✉ Theatre Lane, Lower Glentworth Street ☎ 061-418749 🕐 Dinner Tue–Sat

Mortell's (€)
Fish and chips in Limerick can only mean Mortell's. It's a simple café, but it serves only the best local catch.

✉ 49 Roches Street ☎ 061-415457 🕐 Lunch Mon–Sat

NEW ROSS, CO WATERFORD
The Galley Cruising Restaurant (€€€)
Cruising restaurants ply the waters of the rivers Barrow and Nore from New Ross and Waterford, offering a wonderfully relaxing way to eat and enjoy the scenery at the same time. The *St Ciaran* and *St Brendan* can carry 70 or 80 diners. Lunch, afternoon tea and dinner cruises are all available. Reservations essential.

✉ The Quay, New Ross ☎ 051-421723; www.rivercruise.ie 🕐 Apr–Oct

WATERFORD, CO WATERFORD
Fitzpatrick's (€€–€€€)
A beautifully restored house is home to this Gallic-flavoured fine restaurant, where seafood is the speciality.

✉ Cork Road ☎ 051-378851 🕐 Lunch, dinner

SHOPPING

ANTIQUES
Carol's Antiques
Furniture, silver, china and *objets d'art*.

✉ Main Street, Adare, Co Limerick ☎ 061-396977

George Stackpole
Antiques and books, bought and sold.

✉ Main Street, Adare, Co Limerick ☎ 061-396409

CRAFTS
Black Abbey Crafts
Good selection of quality Irish crafts, including ceramics, slate, iron and glass items.

✉ Adare, Co Limerick ☎ 061-396021 ⏱ Mon–Sat 10–6

Blarney Woollen Mills
First established in 1750, the company now offers woven rugs and Aran sweaters, plus crystal, china and gifts.

✉ Blarney, Co Cork ☎ 021-451 6111

Louis Mulcahy Pottery
This renowned pottery sells quality hand-painted lampshades, sculpted masks, dinner services and much more.

✉ Clogher Head, West Dingle, Co Kerry ☎ 066-915 6229; www.louismulcahy.com ⏱ Jun–Aug daily 9–8; Sep–May daily 9–6

MARKETS
The English Market
Covered market with array of food stalls daily.

✉ Princes Street/Patrick Street/Grand Parade, Cork, Co Cork

Milk Market
Retail outlets open all week; arts and crafts market on Friday; traditional market Saturday morning.

✉ Corn Market Row, Limerick, Co Limerick

SHOPPING CENTRES
Arthur's Quay Shopping Centre
Very attractive collection of over 30 stores in a prime city-centre location; restaurants, day nursery, play area and plenty of parking.

✉ Limerick, Co Limerick

Killarney Outlet Centre
✉ Fair Hill, Killarney

Merchant's Quay Shopping Centre
✉ 1 Patrick Street, Cork, Co Cork

TRADITIONAL MUSIC
Living Tradition
The music shop of Ossian Music Company. Traditional instruments, sheet music, CDs, cassettes, DVDs and videos.
✉ 40 MacCurtain Street, Cork, Co Cork ☎ 021-450 2040

The Sounds of Music
Good range of CDs including traditional Irish music and a selection of instruments.
✉ Henry Street, Kenmare, Co Kerry ☎ 064-42268

Variety Sounds
A wide range of guitars, *bodhráns*, whistles, CDs and books.
✉ 7 College Street, Killarney, Co Kerry ☎ 064-35755

ENTERTAINMENT

LIVE MUSIC
Crowley's
If it's tradition you are seeking you'll find it here in the heart of Kenmare. Impromptu Irish music sessions take place regularly.
✉ Henry Street, Kenmare, Co Kerry ☎ 064-41472

De Barra's Pub
Famous landmark pub featuring live folk and traditional music.
✉ Pearse Street, Clonakilty, Co Cork ☎ 023-33381

Dingle An Droichead Beag
Dingle's musical centre.
✉ Main Street, Dingle, Co Kerry ☎ 066-915 1723

Lobby Bar
Traditional music of Ireland and elsewhere. Concert venue upstairs.
✉ 1 Union Quay, Cork, Co Cork ☎ 021-431 1113

The Old Oak Bar
Top music venue in Cork. Live bands and traditional sessions on two floors.
✉ 113 Oliver Plunkett Street, Cork, Co Cork ☎ 021-427 6165

The Warehouse
Live music venue, located behind a pub which has traditional music and dancing.
✉ Behind Dolan's Pub, Alphonsus Street, off Dock Road, Limerick, Co Limerick ☎ 061-314483

NIGHTCLUB
Newport
Late-night funky lounge and adjacent nightclub.
✉ Paul Street Plaza, Cork, Co Cork ☎ 021-425 4872; 021-425 4874

THEATRE AND CINEMA
Beltable Arts Centre
A venue for theatre, concerts, dance, mime and poetry.
✉ 69 O'Connell Street, Limedrick, Co Limerick ☎ 061-319866

Cinemax
✉ The Quay, Limerick, Co Limerick ☎ 027-55777; www.cinemaxbantry.com

Siamsa Tire – The National Folk Theatre of Ireland
Keeping the national traditions alive.
✉ Town Park, Tralee, Co Kerry ☎ 066-712 3055

Theatre Royal
Hosts the Opera Festival and The Waterford Show.
✉ The Mall, Waterford, Co Waterford ☎ 051-874402

Triskal Arts Centre
Drama, readings, children's theatre and music.
✉ Tobin Street, Cork, Co Cork ☎ 021-427 2022

The West

The wild beauty of the west is underlaid with the hostility of a landscape that does its best to defy cultivation. There are fields, but they are the size of pocket handkerchiefs, and the drystone walls that enclose them have by no means used up all of the land's loose rocks.

Galway

Vast empty areas of blanket bog have pockets of wetness that expand into a network of lakes and rivers beneath the mountains of Connemara and Joyce's Country. The great Loughs – Conn, Mask and Corrib – lie between Sligo and Galway bays. Farther east the River Shannon forms the backbone of a watery highway. In Clare, The Burren is a moonscape of bare limestone, where plants cling on to the sparse soil, and the western boundary of all this is a jagged and spectacular coastline.

GALWAY

Galway, the historic capital of Connaught, is Ireland's fourth largest city, with a delightful blend of ancient and modern. It has at its heart a maze of narrow streets, lined with a mixture of modern shopfronts, traditional-style painted facades, old pubs and restaurants. A relaxed west-coast atmosphere prevails, enlivened by an energetic student population.

Situated in the northeast corner of Galway Bay, where the River Corrib pours into the sea, Galway was built on international trade and sea fishing, and its oldest parts cluster around the harbour and riverside quays. On the east bank is the Spanish Arch, built to protect cargoes of wine and brandy from Iberia. Behind the quay is a network of narrow streets, leading off from the main thorough-fare. A modern shopping mall, incorporating part of the medieval city wall, is hidden away behind old facades. On the far side of the river is The Claddagh, once a close-knit Gaelic-speaking fishing community and now remembered in the continuing tradition of the Claddagh ring, with two hands holding a crowned heart.

Apart from its own attractions, Galway is a good base for exploring the surrounding areas – Connemara, Lough Corrib, the Aran Islands and the Burren.

Salthill is Galway's seaside resort suburb, to the west, offering a good range of amusements and a popular long sandy beach.

www.irelandwest.ie

➕ 17G

ℹ️ Tourist Information ☎ 091-537700

Cathedral of Our Lady Assumed into Heaven and St Nicholas

Overlooking the River Corrib near the Salmon Weir Bridge, this splendid modern Roman Catholic cathedral opened in 1965 and looked so grand that the locals dubbed it the 'Taj Michael', after the then Bishop of Galway, Michael (pronounced Mee-hawl) Brown. Built on the site of the former county gaol (jail), it's topped by a great copper dome, and the interior is plain but impressive, with floors of Connemara marble, rough-hewn limestone walls and superb stained glass. It was designed by John J Robinson and replaced the old cathedral on Abbeygate Street, which has been converted into shops.

✉ University and Gaol roads ☎ 091-563577 🕑 Daily 8:30–6:30 ✋ Free (donations welcome) 🍴 Restaurant (€–€€)

Nora Barnacle House Museum

Built around the end of the 19th century, this tiny cottage now houses one of the smallest museums in Ireland. It was formerly the home of the eponymous Nora Barnacle, companion, wife and lifelong inspiration of the writer James Joyce. He is said to have based the character of Molly Bloom in his novel *Ulysses* on her. Even without the collections of memorabilia, it is impossible to ignore the romantic associations.

www.norabarnacle.com

✉ 8 Bowling Green ☎ 091-564743 🕑 Mid-May to mid-Sep Mon–Sat 10–5 ✋ Inexpensive

St Nicholas's Church

St Nicholas's Church is the largest medieval parish church in Ireland still in constant use. It was built around 1320 by the Lynch family and consecrated to the patron saint of sailors. Christopher Columbus worshipped here in 1477, and was no doubt inspired by tales of St Brendan the Navigator, an Irish monk who sailed to America in the 6th century. Outside the church, on the site of the former college, there is a colourful weekly Saturday market where crafts, organic vegetables and food are sold. In addition to its regular services, St Nicholas's hosts concerts throughout the year.

✉ Market Street ☎ 091-563081 🕑 Daily 11–5; check for services

a walk around Galway

*From Eyre
Square, the heart
of the city, walk
along William
Street, Shop
Street and High
Street. At
the cobbled
crossroads walk
straight on along
Quay Street.*

On the corner is
Thomas Dillon's
Claddagh Gold, a
little jeweller's shop
with a Claddagh
Ring Museum in the
back room. At the
end is the famous
Spanish Arch, where
Iberian traders
would land their
cargoes, behind
which is the new
Galway City
Museum.

*Take the riverside
path that leads off between the bridge and Jury's Hotel.
Cross the next road and continue alongside the river on
your left, and a canal on your right. At the end of the
path, cross a footbridge over the canal, then turn left and
walk to the Salmon Weir Bridge. Cross the bridge and*

the Cathedral of Our Lady Assumed into Heaven and St Nicholas is immediately ahead.

The cathedral, completed in 1965, is topped by a great copper dome. The interior is light, spacious and, though plain, is still very impressive.

Recross the bridge and turn right down Newtown Smith, passing the footbridge crossed earlier. Walk straight on, turn right at the crossroads, then at the end bear left. About halfway along on the right is the Nora Barnacle House Museum.

This tiny cottage is where the writer James Joyce courted his future wife. Mementoes of the couple are on display.

At the end, opposite St Nicholas's Church, turn left into Market Street, then right into Upper Abbeygate Street.

The building at the end, on the right, is Lynch's Castle, now the Allied Irish Bank.

Turn left into William Street and return to Eyre Square.

Distance About 2km (1.2 miles)
Time 2–3 hours
Start/end point Eyre Square
🚌 All city-centre buses
Lunch McDonagh's Seafood House
(€–€€€) ✉ 22 Quay Street
☎ 091-565001 🕐 Seafood Bar:
Mon–Sat 12–9:45, Sun from 5pm
(2pm in summer). Fish and chips:
Mon–Sat noon–midnight, Sun 5–11

More to see in the South

BUNRATTY CASTLE AND FOLK PARK

Bunratty, 14.5km (9 miles) northeast of Limerick, is Ireland's most complete medieval castle, thanks to the restoration work carried out in 1960 when it was purchased by Bord Failte and Lord Gort. Following the restoration, Lord Gort installed his collections of furniture, *objets d'art*, paintings and tapestries, all of which predate 1650. The castle is famous for its medieval banquets, with historic costume and traditional food and entertainment.

In the castle grounds, Irish village life at the turn of the 20th century has been recreated, with reconstructed urban and rural dwellings, farmhouses, a watermill, forge and village street, complete with shops and a pub – all brought to life by

knowledgeable costumed guides. The Regency walled garden and agricultural museum are added attractions.

🚩 17J ✉ N18 Bunratty ☎ 061-360788 ⏰ Daily 9–5:30 (until 7pm Jun–Aug). Last admission 45 mins before closing ✋ Expensive 🍴 Tea room (€); lunches in barn May–Oct (€); Mac's Pub (€€) 🚌 From Limerick, Ennis and Galway 🚆 Limerick and Ennis

THE BURREN AND AILLWEE CAVE

The Burren National Park preserves a remarkable landscape. It is a vast plateau of limestone hills which were scraped free of their soil by retreating glaciers 15,000 years ago, then eroded by rain and Atlantic mists. The tiny amounts of soil that gather in the rock fissures support both Alpine and Mediterranean plant life, and early summer is the main flowering season. **The Burren Centre** provides an overview of the area and its unique landscape, its human history and its famous flora. **Aillwee Cave,** south of Ballyvaughan, has fossil formations and water figures. The Burren is best appreciated on foot, and the waymarked 42km (26-mile) Burren Way, running from Ballyvaughan and Liscannor, can be undertaken in short sections.

🚩 17H (The Burren); 16G (Aillwee Cave)

Burren Centre

✉ Ballyvaughan ☎ 065-707 7277 ⏰ Mid-Mar to Oct daily 10–5 (Jun–Aug 9:30–6) ✋ Moderate

Aillwee Cave

✉ Ballyvaughan ☎ 065-707 7036 ⏰ Tours only: daily from 10am, last tour 5:30 (Jul and 6 Aug); Dec by appointment only ✋ Expensive

CASTLEBAR

Castlebar is the county town of Co Mayo. Its most notable attraction is the **Museum of Country Life.** Housed in a renovated 18th-century building, along with purpose-built extensions and grounds, this is the first branch of the National Museum to be located outside Dublin. Displays utilizing 50,000 items reflect the lives of Ireland's people and their trades, illustrating the social history of Ireland over the past 200 years.

➕ 4E

Museum of Country Life

✉ Turlough Park House ☎ 094-903 1755; www.museum.ie
🕐 Tue–Sat 10–5, Sun 2–5 🍴 Restaurant

CLIFFS OF MOHER

These towering cliffs rise sheer out of the turbulent Atlantic to a height of nearly 213m (700ft) and stretch for 8km (5 miles) along the Clare coast north of Hag's Head. Majestic in calm weather, the cliffs are most dramatic (and dangerous) when stormy seas crash into their base, hurling pebbles high up into the air. Horizontal layers of flagstones have been exposed by coastal erosion, making ideal perches for the sea birds, including puffins, which abound here. At the highest point of the cliffs, **O'Brien's Tower** was constructed in the early 19th century as a lookout point for the first tourists, and gives views of the Clare coastline, the Oileáin Árann (Aran Islands) and mountains as far apart as Kerry and Connemara. A controversial, state-of-the-art visitor centre opened in 2007.

➕ 16H

O'Brien's Tower and Visitor Centre

✉ Near Liscannor ☎ 065-708 1565 🕐 Tower: Mar–Oct 9:30–5:30. Visitor Centre: Jun–Aug daily 8:30–8:30; May, Sep daily 8:30–7; Oct daily 8:30–6; Mar–Apr daily 9–6; Nov–Feb daily 9–5 ✋ Inexpensive; nearby parking €8 per car 🍴 Restaurant (€–€€) 🚌 From Lahinch and other nearby towns

CLONMACNOISE

Best places to see, ➤ 38–39.

CONNEMARA

To the northwest of Galway City is Connemara, with some of the most dramatic scenery in Ireland. Much of its convoluted

coastline, with masses of tiny islands and some excellent beaches, can be followed by road and the views are spectacular. Inland, in southern Connemara, are thousands of lakes amid the bogland. Farther north, and hardly ever out of sight, are the brooding ranges of the Twelve Pins and the Maumturk Mountains. Connemara marble is quarried at Recess, and there is a factory shop and showroom at Connemara Marble Industries in Moycullen. The Connemara National Park protects about 2,000ha (4,940 acres) of the mountains, bogs, heaths and grasslands.

There's a good **visitor centre** in Letterfrack and a herd of Connemara ponies.

www.connemaranationalpark.ie

✚ 3F

National Park Visitor Centre

✉ Letterfrack ☎ 095-41054 🕐 Jul–Aug daily 9:30–6; Jul daily 10–6; Sep to mid-Oct, Apr–May daily 10–5:30 💰 Inexpensive 🍴 Tea rooms (€) ❓ Guided walks Jun–Aug. Talks and special events for children

a drive

around the coast, lakes and mountains of Connemara

This drive follows the coastline for much of the way, with views of the Oileáin Árann (Aran Islands) in the early stages. It then passes through isolated settlements amid a rocky landscape, with mountain views, to end at the lovely little town of Clifden.

From Galway follow signs for Salthill until you reach a roundabout on the seafront, then take the Spiddal road west along Galway Bay. At the T-junction turn left, signposted Carraroe and Barna, then after about 13km (8 miles) pass through Spiddal.

There are breathtaking views along the coast and across Galway Bay before the road swings right to open up an inland vista of distant mountains.

Turn right onto the R336, signed 'Cill Ciarain, Scriob, Carna and Ros Muc'. After 11km 7 miles) at a T-junction, turn left signed 'Connemara Scenic Route'. Continue through Cill Ciarain (Kilkieran). After 8.5km (5 miles) bear right, signed 'Clifden', with views of the Twelve Pins ahead. Turn left onto the R342 and follow signs for Roundstone.

This charming village is the home of Malachy Kearns' *bodrhán* workshop, where the craftsman can often be seen making his famous traditional Irish drums. There is also a pottery close by.

After 13km (8 miles) reach Ballyconneely and continue around the rocky bay, then turn left into Clifden after a further 9km (5.5 miles).

If you want to complete the circle, the road back to Galway (about 48km/30 miles) is well signposted.

Distance 112km (70 miles)
Time About 5 hours, including stop for lunch and visits to craft workshops
Start point Galway ✚ 17G
End point Clifden ✚ 2F
Lunch O'Dowds Seafood Restaurant (€€–€€€, ➤ 156)
✉ Roundstone ☎ 095-35809

KNAPPOGUE CASTLE

Built in the mid-15th century for the MacNamara family, Knappogue underwent many changes over the course of the next five centuries. It was extended and adapted and used as government offices for a while, before falling into a ruinous state. In the 1960s it was acquired by Mark Edwin Andrews, then Assistant Secretary to the US Navy. He and his wife set about the task of restructuring the castle into an authentic setting for the medieval banquets which continue to be popular. They include dinner and a pageant, with stories of the history of the women of Ireland – real and legendary. The castle was acquired by the Shannon Development Company in 1996.

🚹 17H ✉ Kilmurry, near Quin ☎ 061-360788 ③ Apr–Oct daily 9:30–5 (last admission 1 hour before closing) ✋ Moderate ❓ Medieval banquets on demand

KYLEMORE ABBEY

Kylemore Abbey's greatest attraction is its location. Nestled at the base of Duchruach Mountain, and on the north shores of Lough Pollacapul in the heart of the Connemara Mountains, it is regarded as one of Ireland's most romantic buildings. Lying in a rhododendron-filled hollow, this neo-Gothic estate castle was constructed for British shipping magnate and Irish politican Mitchell Henry. Since 1920 it has been a convent of the Irish Benedictine nuns, and a girls' boarding school now occupies the building. It offers the warmth and hospitality of its peaceful setting to visitors from all over the world. The restaurant has the best of home cooking and a range of the abbey's distinctive pottery can be seen in the studio. Within the grounds there is a Gothic chapel, which has a Connemara marble interior. Nearby is a *taghallai*, a pre-Christian tomb. The 2.5ha (6-acre) restored Victorian walled garden is well worth a visit, as is the visitor centre.

www.kylemoreabbey.com

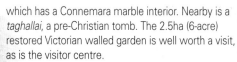 2F ✉ Connemara ☎ 095-41146 ☻ Visitor Centre: daily 9–5. Gardens: mid-Mar to Oct daily 10–4:30. Closed Christmas week and Good Friday ✋ Expensive 🍴 Restaurant (€–€€) 🚌 No bus

OILEÁIN ÁRANN (ARAN ISLANDS)
Best places to see, ➤ 50–51.

THE SHANNON
Ireland's longest river, the Shannon rises in a humble pool (called the Shannon Pot) in Co Cavan, then gathers strength as it flows through a series of lakes before it meets the Atlantic beyond Limerick. Historically, river crossings were always points where towns grew and prospered. Places such as Carrick-on-Shannon and Athlone are bases for leisure cruiser holidays for which this mighty river is so popular.

✚ 16J

ℹ Shannon Development ☎ 061-361555

SLIGO

Sligo is a lively and attractive town with splendid old shopfronts and traditional music pubs. It is also a significant cultural centre and has a fine range of art galleries and museums, as well as the various festivals which take place throughout the year.

Over 1,000 years of history have shaped the town, but it is literature that attracts many of its visitors. This is Yeats country, and the subject of one of his best-known poems is just outside the town – the Isle of Inisfree in Lough Gill (riverboat trips to the lough depart from Sligo's Doorly Park). Sligo also has two fine cathedrals and Sligo Abbey, a Dominican friary founded in 1252.

🚏 5D

ℹ️ Temple Street ☎ 071-916 1201

WESTPORT

Set on Clew Bay, Westport is one of the liveliest and most charming towns in the west of Ireland, with broad Georgian streets and a leafy riverside avenue at its heart. Nearby **Westport House** dates from the 1730s and is the only stately home open to the public in Sligo. It is beautifully furnished and has some superb Waterford crystal, silver and paintings. The dungeons are from an earlier building, reputedly a castle of

Grace O'Malley, the 16th-century pirate queen, and the grounds contain a miniature railway and amusements for children.

✚ 3E

Westport House

✉ The Quay, Westport ☎ 098-25430/27766; www.westporthouse.ie
🕓 Mid-Mar to Sep daily 11:30–5:30; Oct Sat–Sun 11:30–5.30. Amusements Easter and Jun–Aug 👆 Expensive 🍴 Café Jun, Aug only (€)

YEATS TOWER, THOOR BALLYLEE

In 1917 the poet William Butler Yeats bought this derelict 16th-century tower house and renovated it. For the next 12 years he and his family spent their summers here and it was in these peaceful surroundings that he wrote most of his works. His life-long friend and patron, Lady Gregory, lived nearby, and

together they were the inspiration behind the Irish Literary Revival and the founding of the Abbey Theatre in Dublin (▶ 110). In

the 1960s Thoor Ballylee was again restored, to show how it looked when Yeats was here, and was opened to the public.

✚ 17G ✉ Gort ☎ 091-631436 (off season 091-537700) 🕓 May–Sep daily 10–6
👆 Moderate ❓ Audio-visual presentation and displays of first editions. Bookshop, craft centre, picnic area

HOTELS

BALLYVAUGHAN, CO CLARE
Drumcreehy House (€)
Just 1.5km (1 mile) north of the village and across the road from the sea, this bed-and-breakfast has character and style, with German and Irish antiques everywhere.
✉ Ballyvaughan ☎ 065-707 7377; www.drumcreehyhouse.com

BUNRATTY, CO CLARE
Bunratty Woods Country House (€–€€)
Situated in the grounds of Bunratty Castle, this guest house contains many interesting antiques and has mountain views.
✉ Low Road ☎ 061-369689 ◷ Closed 7 Nov–early Mar

CASHEL, CO GALWAY
Cashel House (€€€)
Gracious country-house hotel in superb gardens overlooking Cashel Bay.
✉ Off the N59, 1.5km (1 mile) west of Recess ☎ 095-31001; www.cashel-house-hotel.com ◷ Closed early Jan–early Feb

CASTLEREA, CO ROSCOMMON
Clonalis House (€€€)
Clonalis House is the home of the O'Conors of Connacht, descendants of the Kings of Connacht and the last High King of Ireland. Guests here can browse through old family manuscripts and see the harp which belonged to the great Turlough O'Carolan.
✉ On the west side of Castlerea on the N60 ☎ 949-620014; www.clonalis.com ◷ Closed Oct to mid-Apr

DOOLIN, CO CLARE
Aran View House (€–€€)
This comfortable hotel is set in farmland, with views of the Aran Islands.
✉ Coast Road ☎ 065-707 4061; www.aranview.com ◷ Closed end Oct–Easter

GALWAY, CO GALWAY
Glenlo Abbey (€€€)
Occupying an 18th-century abbey in a landscaped estate overlooking a lough.

✉ Bushypark ☎ 091-526666; www.glenlo.com

White House (€–€€)
A guest house overlooking Galway Bay and The Burren, the White House has large, well-equipped bedrooms.

✉ 2 Ocean Wave, Salthill ☎ 091-529399; www.white-house-hotel.com

ROUNDSTONE, CO GALWAY
Eldon's (€–€€)
A distinctive blue-and-yellow painted building in this picturesque fishing village. Eldon's restaurant specializes in local seafood.

✉ Main Street ☎ 095-35933; www.eldons.ie ⏰ Closed Jan

RESTAURANTS

BALLYVAUGHAN, CO CLARE
Hyland's Burren Hotel (€–€€)
Located close to the harbour, the hotel offers an excellent range of dishes. There is a popular bar menu for lunches.

✉ Ballyvaughan ☎ 065-707 7037; www.hylandsburren.com ⏰ Lunch, dinner; closed Jan–Feb

Monks Bar & Restaurant (€€)
Renowned for its seafood chowder, Monks is a seafood speciality restaurant overlooking Galway Bay.

✉ Old Pier, Ballyvaughan ☎ 065-707 7059; www.monks.ie ⏰ Lunch, dinner

CLARENBRIDGE, CO GALWAY
Paddy Burke's (€€)
Famous as the focal point of the Clarenbridge Oyster Festival; no prizes for guessing the speciality dish.

✉ Clarenbridge ☎ 091-796226; www.paddyburkesgalway.com ⏰ Lunch, dinner; closed Good Fri and 25 Dec

CLIFDEN, CO GALWAY
Mitchell's (€€)

Hearty Irish stew is the speciality here, with good portions of seafood and steaks from a varied menu.

✉ Market Street ☎ 095-21867 🕐 Lunch, dinner; closed mid-Nov to mid-Mar

GALWAY, CO GALWAY
K C Blakes (€–€€)

John Casey (K C) is the larger-than-life owner of this ultramodern little eatery. Dishes are traditional Irish with a twist.

✉ 10 Quay Street, Spanish Arch ☎ 091-561826 🕐 Lunch, dinner

Kirbys of Cross Street (€–€€)

Good-value contemporary cuisine on Irish themes, seasoned with influences from further afield.

✉ Cross Street ☎ 091-569404; www.kirbysrestaurant.com 🕐 Lunch, dinner

Kirwan's Lane Restaurant (€€–€€€)

Stylish modern restaurant serving bistro-type grills and Asian-influenced dishes..

✉ Kirwan's Lane ☎ 091-568266 🕐 Mon–Sat lunch, dinner, Sun dinner only; closed 25 Dec

Trattoria Pasta Mista (€–€€)

You'll find fresh home-made pasta and traditional Italian dishes at this lively trattoria in the heart of the city.

✉ 12 Quay Street ☎ 091-563910 🕐 Dinner; call to check lunch times

KILCOLGAN, CO GALWAY
Morans Oyster Cottage (€–€€€)

Famous for its seafood. Specialities include chowder and smoked salmon.

✉ The Weir ☎ 091-796113; www.moransoystercottage.com
🕐 Lunch, dinner

LETTERFRACK, CO GALWAY
Rosleague Manor (€€€)
You have to make a reservation to eat in the classy restaurant of this stunning Georgian house, set in 12ha (30 acres) overlooking Ballinakill Bay. Seafood is the speciality.
✉ Letterfrack ☎ 095-41101; www.rosleague.com 🕐 Lunch, dinner; closed Nov to mid-Mar

LISDOONVARNA, CO CLARE
Sheedy's Country House Hotel (€€€)
Set in lovely gardens, this family-run hotel-restaurant has an excellent reputation for its food and hospitality.
✉ Lisdoonvarna ☎ 065-707 4026; www.sheedys.com 🕐 Lunch (bar meals), dinner; closed mid-Oct to Easter

MOYCULLEN, CO GALWAY
White Gables Restaurant (€€€)
This charming restaurant has an excellent reputation for its French cuisine and seafood.
✉ Moycullen village ☎ 091-555744; www.whitegables.com 🕐 Dinner Mon–Sat, lunch Sun only; closed 23 Dec to mid-Feb

OILEÁIN ÁRANN (ARAN ISLANDS), CO GALWAY
Mainistir House (€)
Come here for a quirky dining experience overlooking the bay. The daily changing set menu is sure to please.
✉ Inis Mór (Inishmore) ☎ 099-61169 🕐 Daily: dinner at 8pm (one sitting only)

RECESS, CO GALWAY
Ballynahinch Castle (€€–€€€)
Local game, fish and fresh produce inspire the menu here.
✉ On Roundstone road, off N59, 5km (3 miles) west of Recess ☎ 095-31006; www.ballynahinch-castle.com 🕐 Lunch (bar meals), dinner; closed 29 Jan–23 Feb and 15–27 Dec

ROUNDSTONE, CO GALWAY

O'Dowd's Seafood Restaurant (€€–€€€)

Traditional pub with restaurant serving excellent Irish cooking prepared using fresh locally caught fish.

✉ Roundstone ☎ 095-35809; www.odowdsbar.com ⏲ Lunch, dinner

SLIGO, CO SLIGO

Embassy Rooms and The Belfry (€–€€)

Renowned for both its à la carte and its bar food.

✉ John F Kennedy Parade ☎ 071-916 1250; www.belfrypub.com ⏲ Lunch, dinner; closed Good Fri, 25 Dec

Fiddlers Creek (€€–€€€)

Good, wholesome steak and fish dishes served with an interesting slant. Some tables overlook the river.

✉ Rockwood Parade ☎ 071-914 1866 ⏲ Dinner daily; lunch Sun only

WESTPORT, CO MAYO

Asgard Bar and Restaurant (€€–€€€)

Overlooking Clew Bay; good seafood and Irish specialities.

✉ The Quay ☎ 098-25319 ⏲ Lunch, dinner; closed Mon and Tue off season

SHOPPING

CRAFTS

Ballycasey Craft & Design Centre

Craftspeople here include potters, a goldsmith, a florist and more.

✉ Shannon, Co Clare ☎ 061-364115

Burren Perfumery

Demonstrations, displays, photographic exhibition and tea rooms.

✉ Carron, Co Clare ☎ 065-708 9102 ⏲ Daily 9–5 (until 7pm Jun–Sep); sometimes closed Jan

Doolin Crafts Gallery

Crafts gallery run by batik artist and jewellery designer. Also sells weaving and Irish instruments. Restaurant serving local produce.

✉ Doolin, Co Clare ☎ 065-707 4309 ⏲ Daily (restaurant Apr–Oct)

Foxford Woollen Mills Visitor Centre

Take a tour of the historic woollen mill. Also houses jewellery and woodcraft workshops and an art gallery.

✉ Foxford, Co Mayo ☎ 094-925 6104

IDA Centre

Music, fashion and craft shops including pottery and jewellery. *Bodhrán*-making demonstrations. Café.

✉ Roundstone, Co Galway ☎ 095-35875

Tús Craft Design Shop

This craft co-op centre displays ceramics, stained glass, painted silks, jewellery and delightful fairy dolls.

✉ Bridge Mills, Bridge Street, Galway, Co Galway ☎ 091-532500
🕐 Mon–Sat 10–6

DEPARTMENT STORES

Brown Thomas

A western version of Dublin's most stylish shop. The place for luxury, perfume, designer clothes and accessory shopping.

✉ 18–21 Eglinton Buildings, Galway ☎ 091-565254 🕐 Mon–Sat 9:30–7 (until 8pm Thu and Fri), Sun 12–6

Penneys

Fashion for everyone; good accessories department and household wares.

✉ Eyre Square Centre, Galway, Co Galway ☎ 091-566889/565095

TRADITIONAL MUSIC

Custy's Traditional Music Shop

Owned and staffed by experts. A real gem.

✉ Francis Street, Ennis, Co Clare ☎ 065-682 1727

Mulligans

Stocks just about every traditional Irish music recording ever made; also jazz, blues, soul and country music.

✉ 5 Middle Street, Galway, Co Galway ☎ 091-564961

ENTERTAINMENT

LIVE MUSIC

Bar Cuba

Latin American and jazz.

✉ Eyre Square, Galway, Co Galway ☎ 091-565991

The Roisin Dubh

Traditional Irish, rock and pop in pub and on stage.

✉ 8 Upper Dominick Street, Galway, Co Galway ☎ 091-586540 🕐 Nightly

Tigh Colí

Traditional music venue.

✉ Mainguard Street, Galway, Co Galway ☎ 091-561294 🕐 Nightly at 5:30 and 10pm

NIGHTCLUBS

Beo

Live bands and DJs draw in the crowds at this Salthill venue.

✉ O'Connor's Warwick Hotel, Salthill, Co Galway ☎ 091-521244 🕐 Fri, Sat from 11pm

GPO

Definitely the hippest and most popular dance club in the West.

✉ Eglington Street, Galway, Co Galway ☎ 091-563073 🕐 Mon–Wed 10pm–2am, Thu–Sun 11pm–3am

THEATRE AND CINEMA

Claddagh Hall

Traditional music and dance and folk drama.

✉ Nimmos Pier, Galway, Co Galway ☎ 091-755479/588044/755888

🕐 Mid-Jun to early Sep 8:45pm

Galway Omniplex

Premier cinema complex with the latest technology in projection and sound.

✉ Headford Road, Galway, Co Galway ☎ 091-567800

The North

The end of 'The Troubles' in Northern Ireland has seen a mini economic boom and a sudden influx of new tourists to what is one of the most underrated parts of Ireland. Its beautiful scenery can match anything down south, but much of the region still feels undiscovered, and this only adds to the excitement of a visit and the warmness of the welcome you'll receive.

The coast of Antrim offers a spectacular drive past the lovely

Glens before swinging west to the Giant's Causeway.

Further south the Mountains of Mourne sweep down to the sea. Inland are forest parks, lakes and mountains, historic towns, ancient sites and, of course, Belfast, a busy city with an industrial heritage and a lively arts scene. This section also includes the far northwestern part of the Republic, Co Donegal, famous for its beaches and tweed.

BELFAST

The capital of Northern Ireland is a relatively young city that grew rapidly in Victorian times, when its linen and shipbuilding industries flourished and the city doubled in size every 10 years. Today it has a unique character, brought about by the combination of hard work, hard times and a particular brand of Irish humour. The redevelopment of its dockyard areas continues to breathe new life and prosperity into the eastern flank of the city centre.

Belfast's industrial past, together with the disturbing images of the recent troubles, can conjure up a somewhat misleading picture for those who have never visited the city. Its Victorian prosperity has left a legacy of magnificent public buildings and monuments, finance houses and warehouses. At the heart of the city is the spacious and leafy Donegall Square, dominated by the magnificent City Hall, and the whole area is undergoing a huge makeover.

Belfast has superb museums, libraries and art galleries, excellent shopping and a lively and varied cultural life, from grand opera to informal traditional music sessions.

Beautiful parks and gardens include the famous Botanic Gardens and the canalside Lagan Valley Regional Park, but the most spectacular is on the slopes of Cave Hill to the north, which incorporates the zoo, Belfast Castle and a heritage centre.

✚ 10C

🛈 59 North Street ☎ 028 9023 1221

Botanic Gardens

The Botanic Gardens are a wonderful place to wander away from the bustle of the city. It includes a fragrant rose garden, formal beds and herbaceous borders, and among the outstanding greenhouses is the Palm House. Begun in 1839, it is a remarkable cast-iron curvilinear structure in which tropical flowering plants thrive. Also in these lovely surroundings, the **Ulster Museum** gives a fascinating insight into the life and history of the Province. 'Made in Belfast' underlines the industry and inventiveness of Ulster (Northern Ireland) people, and there are many displays including 'Early Ireland' (10,000BC–1500BC).

✚ *Belfast 1f (off map)* ✉ Stranmills Road ☎ 028 9032 4902 ⏰ Palm House: Apr–Sep Mon–Fri 10–5, Sat–Sun 2–5; Oct–Mar Mon–Fri 10–4, Sat–Sun 2–4. Closes for lunch ✋ Free 🚌 84, 85 🚉 Botanic Station

Ulster Museum

☎ 028 9038 3000; www.ulstermuseum.org.uk ⏰ Closed for renovation until the beginning of 2009 ✋ Free

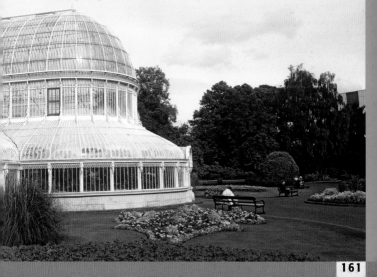

City Hall

In 1906 Belfast's City Hall was completed to mark the granting of city status by Queen Victoria. Set around a central courtyard, the building, of Portland stone, is topped by a tall copper dome which rises above the central staircase at the heart of an exuberant interior of rich mosaic, stained glass, marble and wood panelling.

✚ *Belfast 2d* ✉ Donegall Square ☎ 028 9027 0456 ⏰ Tours: Jun–Sep Mon–Fri 11, 2, 3, Sat 2:30; Oct–May Mon–Fri 11, 2:30, Sat 2:30 ✋ Free

Crown Liquor Saloon

High Victorian decor is preserved in this pub, in the care of the National Trust. It's a working pub managed by a brewery. The tiled exterior, with Corinthian pillars flanking the doorway, gives way to marble counters, stained glass, gleaming brass and ornately carved 'snugs'.

✚ *Belfast 1e* ✉ Great Victoria Street ☎ 028 9027 9901 ⏰ Mon–Sat 11:30–12, Sun 11:30–10 ✋ Free

Odyssey

Belfast's big millennium project was the building of this complex covering 9ha (23 acres) of the riverfront. It includes an interactive science centre with a special area for kids under eight, an IMAX theatre, a 12-screen multiplex cinema and a huge arena. The Pavilion has restaurants, bars and shops.

✛ *Belfast 4b* ✉ 2 Queen's Quay ☎ 028 9045 1055 ✋ Varies by attraction

Queen's University

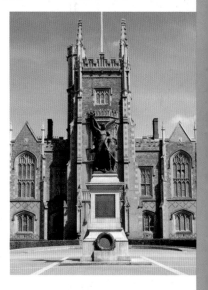

Northern Ireland's leading seat of third-level learning was founded by Queen Victoria and stands right at the heart of the city along eponymous University Road. The elegant, Charles Lanyon designed, redbrick-and-sandstone, Tudor-revival building dates back to 1849, and it's three square towers have long been city landmarks. The university has grown a lot since then, but the enclosed campus is still a joy to stroll around and the Welcome Centre hosts regular exhibitions, as does the Naughton Art Gallery. The Seamus Heaney Library is named after the Nobel Prize-winning poet and alumnus. Guided tours can be arranged in advance.

✛ *Belfast 1f (off map)* ✉ University Road ☎ 028 9033 5252; www.qub.ac.uk ⏰ Welcome Centre: May–Sep Mon–Sat 10–4; Oct–Apr Mon–Fri 10–4 ✋ Free

a walk around Belfast

This walk starts in the heart of the city, then heads south along 'The Golden Mile' to visit the lovely Botanic Gardens and the Ulster Museum.

Donegall Square is surrounded by splendid architecture. Take a look at some of the statues and monuments in the grounds of City Hall before going inside (guided tours can be arranged in advance).

Leave by the exit on the opposite side. Outside the gates of City Hall turn left along Donegall Square South. At the corner cross into May Street, then turn right into Alfred Street. Continue to reach St Malachy's on the left.

Ulster Museum

Pedestrian Entrance

St Malachy's Church was built in 1844 in castellated Gothic style with dark red brick and slender octagonal turrets. Inside there is fine fan-vaulting and an organ by Telford.

From St Malachy's Church enter Clarence Street, turn left into Bedford Street, then bear right into Dublin Road and continue to Shaftesbury Square. Continue along Bradbury Place and fork left into University Road. Beyond the university, turn left to enter the Botanic Garden, where the Ulster Museum can be found.

The beautiful Botanic Gardens feature a great Palm House and Tropical Ravine. Nearby is the excellent Ulster Museum.

Retrace your steps to Shaftesbury Square, then fork left to go along Great Victoria Street, passing the Crown Liquor Saloon on the right.

Try to time the walk so that this famous National Trust pub, with its sumptuous and ornate Victorian interior, will be open.

Continue past the Europa Hotel and the splendid Opera House, then turn right into Howard Street and return to Donegall Square.

Distance About 4km (2.5 miles)
Time 3–4 hours, including cathedral, gardens and museum visits
Start/end point Donegall Square 🚆 *Belfast 2d* 🚌 All city-centre buses
Lunch Crown Liquor Saloon (££, ► 162)

More to see in the North

ARMAGH

Armagh has a heritage of national importance. Nearby Navan Fort was the ancient capital of the kings of Ulster, and in AD445 St Patrick built his first church on the site now occupied by St Patrick's Cathedral. From here the Irish were converted to Christianity and Armagh remains the ecclesiastical capital of Ireland. There has been much rebuilding of this Church of Ireland cathedral, but its core is medieval. There is also a Roman Catholic cathedral of St Patrick, finished in 1904, with a lavish interior of murals depicting Irish saints. **St Patrick's Trian** has an exhibition on the saint, along with the Land of Lilliput featuring Gulliver's travels. St Patrick was born around AD390 in Britain, the son of a Romano-British official. At 16 he was kidnapped by pirates and sold into slavery in Ireland, but later escaped due, he claimed, to divine intervention. This prompted his training for the ministry in Britain, before returning to Ireland and establishing the Christian faith here.

The city has many other beautiful buildings on its old streets, and the stables of the former Archbishop's Palace have been converted into the excellent **Palace Stables Heritage Centre**.

✚ 9D 🚌 From Portadown Station 🚆 Portadown

St Patrick's Trian

www.saintpatrickstrian.com

✉ 40 English Street ☎ 028 3752 1801 🕐 Sep–Jun Mon–Sat 10–5, Sun 2–5; Jul–Aug Mon–Sat 10–5:30, Sun 2–6 💷 Moderate 🍴 Restaurant (£)

Palace Stables Heritage Centre
✉ Friary Road ☎ 028 3752 9629 ⏰ Apr–May, Sep Sat–Sun 10–5; Jun–Aug Mon–Sat 10–5, Sun 12–5 🖐 Moderate 🍴 Coffee shop (£), restaurant (£)

BALLYCASTLE

Ballycastle, Co Antrim's largest town, is a popular seaside resort surrounded by some of Ireland's loveliest scenery. Nearby is the Carrick-a-Rede Rope Bridge, suspended 24.5m (80ft) above the sea, linking the clifftop to a rocky island, and from the harbour there are trips to Rathlin Island, one of the best places for birdwatching in Ireland.

On the edge of the town are the ruins of **Bonamargy Friary,** founded around 1500 and the burial place of the MacDonnell chiefs. At the end of August each year, the Diamond, at the centre of the town, is crammed with stalls, entertainments and horse-dealing during the famous Oul' Lammas Fair. **Ballycastle Museum** is in the 18th-century courthouse, and there's a Seafront Exhibition Centre with crafts and information.

➕ 10A 🚌 From Ballymoney Station
🚆 Ballymoney

Bonamargy Friary
✉ Ballycastle
⏰ All year 🖐 Free

Ballycastle Museum
✉ 59 Castle Street
☎ 028 2076 2942
⏰ Jul–Aug (or by arrangement) Mon–Sat 12–6
🖐 Free

CARRICKFERGUS

Carrickfergus has the country's finest Norman **castle,** built on the edge of the sea in the late 12th century and still in use (as a magazine and armoury) as recently as 1928. Its walls now house three floors of exhibitions, and a medieval fair is held here each July.

There are remains of the 17th-century town walls, the earliest and largest urban defence in Ulster, including the North Gate, which has been rebuilt and restored.

Carrickfergus was the first footfall in Ireland of William of Orange, who landed here in 1690 for his victorious campaign against James II. Billy's Rock reputedly marks the exact spot.

Visit the unusual **Flame! The Gasworks Museum of Ireland,** Ireland's sole surviving coal gasworks, that supplied the town with gas for over 100 years until 1967.

✚ 10C 🚶 Carrickfergus

Carrickfergus Castle

✉ Marine Highway ☎ 028 9335 1273 🕓 Jun–Aug Mon–Sat 10–6, Sun 12–6; Apr, May, Sep Mon–Sat 10–6, Sun 2–6; Oct–Mar Mon–Sat 10–4, Sun 2–4 ✋ Moderate

Flame! The Glassworks Museum of Ireland

✉ 44 Irish Quarter West ☎ 028 9336 9575 🕓 Apr–Jun, Sep daily 2–6; Jul–Aug daily 10–6; Mar, Oct Sat–Sun 2–6 ✋ Inexpensive

DONEGAL

Donegal Tweed has made the name of this northwest corner of Ireland familiar all around the world. It is a modest little town, but it has the remains of two castles and two abbeys, and is attractively set at the head of Donegal Bay. **Donegal Castle,** on the banks of the River Eske in the town centre, was built in 1505 for Red Hugh O'Donnell and was considerably enlarged in the 17th century for

Sir Basil Brooke. The Brooke family also owned Lough Eske Castle, a Jacobean-style house damaged by fire in 1939.

South of the town is **Donegal Abbey**. *The Annals of the Four Masters* was written here in the 17th century, charting the history of Ireland up until 1616. This important chronicle is now in the National Library in Dublin.

➕ 6C

Donegal Castle
✉ Tinchonaill Street ☎ 074-972 2405; www.heritageireland.ie ⏰ Mid-Mar to Oct daily 10–6; Nov to mid-Mar Thu–Mon 9:30–4:30 (last admission 45 mins before closing) 💷 Inexpensive

Donegal Abbey
✉ Donegal ☎ Call Donegal tourist office: 074-972 1148 ⏰ Daily
🍴 Refreshments (£)

ENNISKILLEN

Enniskillen is attractively set on the River Erne between Upper and Lower Lough Erne. **Enniskillen Castle,** built in the early 15th century, was the medieval stronghold of the Maguires and has a picturesque water gate. The keep now houses the Fermanagh Museum and a military museum. St Macartan's Cathedral is a small but interesting building, dating from the early 17th century, with some fine monuments and stained glass.

The Fermanagh Lakelands surrounding Enniskillen provide for all kinds of water-based leisure pursuits, and on Devenish Island is an important monastic site, founded in the 6th century by St Molaise. A little farther afield is **Castle Coole,** designed by James Wyatt in 1795. The interiors are exquisite and the parkland runs down to the shores of Lough Coole. **Florence Court** is to the southwest, an 18th-century mansion noted for its rococo plasterwork.

🔂 7D

🛳 Ferry from Lower Lough Erne, north of Enniskillen, to Devenish Island

Enniskillen Castle

✉ Castle Barracks, Wellington Road ☎ 028 6632 5000; www.enniskillencastle.co.uk 🕔 Mon 2–5, Tue–Fri 10–5. Also open May–Sep Sat 2–5 (also Sun 2–5 Jul–Aug) 👍 Inexpensive 🚌 Ulster Bus Station

Castle Coole

☎ 028 6632 2690; www.nationaltrust.co.uk 🕔 Grounds: May–Sep daily 10–8; Oct–Apr daily 10–4. House: Mar to mid-May, Sep Sat–Sun 12–6; Jun–Aug daily 12–6 (closed Tue in Jun). Last tour 5:15 👍 Moderate 🍽 Refreshments (£) 🚌 Ulsterbus 261 from Belfast to Enniskillen

Florence Court

✉ 12km (7.5 miles) southwest of Enniskillen ☎ 028 6634 8249/8497 🕔 Grounds: May–Sep daily 10–8; Oct–Apr daily 10–4. House: Mar daily 1–6; Apr–May, Sep Sat–Sun 1–6; Jun Wed–Mon 1–6. Closed rest of year 👍 Moderate 🍽 Tea room (£) 🚌 Ulsterbus 192 Enniskillen–Swanlinbar

THE GIANT'S CAUSEWAY

Best places to see, ➤ 42–43.

THE GIANT'S CAUSEWAY COAST

The Giant's Causeway coast encompasses dramatic cliffs, wide sandy beaches, pretty fishing villages and clifftop castles. Portrush, the nearest large town, is a traditional seaside resort with two splendid beaches, and nearby is **Dunluce Castle,** a fairy-tale ruin which seems to grow out of the rock on which it is perched. Portballintrae is a pretty fishing village, made famous by the discovery in 1967 of the most valuable sunken treasure ever found on an Armada wreck – the *Girona* – which foundered here in 1588, with only five survivors from its crew of 1,300. The rescued treasure is now on display and can be seen in Belfast's Ulster Museum (➤ 161).

✚ 9–10A

Dunluce Castle

✉ 87 Dunluce Road, Bushmills ☎ 028 2073 1938; www.northantrim.com
🕐 Jun–Aug Mon–Sat 10–6, Sun 12–6; Apr, May, Sep Mon–Sat 10–5, Sun 2–6; Oct–Mar Mon–Sat 10–4, Sun 2–4 ✋ Inexpensive 🚌 172 Portrush–Ballycastle

THE GLENS OF ANTRIM

There are nine Glens of Antrim, lying roughly east of an imaginary line drawn between Ballycastle and Ballymena, and all of them are beautiful. There are wide valleys with a patchwork of green pastures, densely wooded mountain slopes and rocky gorges with tumbling streams dappled by the sunlight shining through the overhanging trees. Many of the glens are designated nature reserves and there are splendid walks, rich in wildlife and botanical interest and often with views to the coast. Millions of years of geological upheaval have formed these delightful valleys, which lie between the great plateau of the Antrim Mountains and a coastline that is justifiably described as the most scenic in the British Isles (➤ 174–175). Glenariff, the best known, has been dubbed the 'queen of the glens', and there is a wonderful view from the visitor centre.

✚ 10B

ℹ Tourist Information Centre: Sheskburn House, 7 Mary Street, Ballycastle

☎ 028 2076 2024

LETTERKENNY

Letterkenny's long main street is overlooked by the Cathedral of St Eunan, built over 100 years ago and containing some important stained glass. The Donegal County Museum has artefacts from the Stone Age to the medieval period as well as more recent history and folk life. In Church Hill, on the shore of Lough Gartan, the lovely **Glebe House** is an art gallery, and just outside the town on the Glenties road is the Newmills Corn and Flax Mills.

✠ 7B

Glebe House and Gallery

✉ Churchill ☎ 074-913 7071 ⏰ Easter and mid-May to late Sep Sat–Thu 11–6:30 💷 Inexpensive 🍴 Tea room (£)

LONDONDERRY

Londonderry (Derry) is a city that is historically absorbing, yet lively

and modern too. Take a guided walk of about 1.5km (1 mile) around its 17th-century town walls, which are still unbroken in spite of a 105-day siege by Jacobite forces in 1689, one of the most significant battles in Irish history. The city has hardly ever been trouble-free. Ever since St Columba founded his first monastery here in AD546, its accessible location on the Foyle estuary attracted marauders. You can learn more of the history of the town at the **Tower Museum.**

Londonderry has impressive public buildings, two fine cathedrals and dramatic townscapes, but there are also lots of little lanes to explore, and behind the 19th-century Guildhall is the quay from which so many emigrants sailed for the New World.

✠ 8B

Tower Museum

✉ Union Hall Place ☎ 028 7137 2411; www.heritageireland.ie ⏰ Jul–Aug daily 10–4; Mar–Jan Mon–Sat 10–5; rest of year Mon–Thu 10–4 💷 Moderate 🚌 Londonderry

a drive ⊘around the Antrim coast

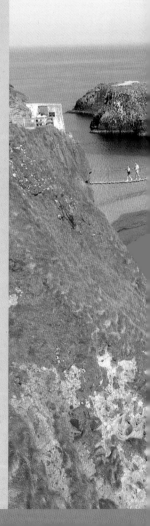

From Larne take the A2 north signed Glenarm and the Antrim Coast Road.

All the way to Ballycastle there is wonderful coastal scenery and pretty villages. Turn off to explore the Glens of Antrim if you have time.

Pass Bonamargy Friary on the left and at the T-junction turn left into Ballycastle. From the Diamond take the A2 signposted 'Portrush, Bushmills, Giant's Causeway'. Soon turn right, signposted 'Ballintoy, B15, Coastal Route'. At the T-junction turn right and continue, passing the turning to Carrick-a-Rede Rope Bridge.

In summer the rope bridge is strung high above the water across the gap between the mainland and a little rocky island.

Go through Ballintoy and after 5.5km (3.5 miles) turn right into Causeway Road. After another 5.5km (3.5 miles) you reach the Visitor Centre.

This is a World Heritage Site and a unique phenomenon which should not be missed.

From the Causeway, take the A2 to Bushmills and at the roundabout in the village go straight over, signposted 'Dervock'. After a short distance, reach the Bushmills Distillery on the left.

Though it is a large-scale working distillery, Bushmills is well prepared for visitors, with an interesting and entertaining tour, tastings and shops.

Continue to Dervock, then at a T-junction turn right with the B66, signposted 'Ballymoney'. About 6.5km (4 miles) farther on turn left onto the A26. Stay on this road and at the end of its short motorway section, reach a roundabout and turn left onto the A36. From here follow signs back to Larne.

Distance 160km (100 miles)
Time About 7 hours
Start/end point Larne ✚ 10B
Lunch Wysner's (£, ➤ 181)
✉ 16 Ann Street, Ballycastle ☎ 028 2076 2372

LOUGH NEAGH

Lough Neagh, the largest lake in the British Isles, has little hidden harbours, sandy beaches and a number of islands. Lakes are always best explored by boat, and Lough Neagh is no exception, because the roads around it rarely follow the waterline. The *Irish Mist* cruises around the lake from the marina at Antrim, a busy and attractive town, with a famous 9th-century round tower.

In the southeastern corner of the lough, Oxford Island has a range of habitats for birdlife, including wet meadows, reedbeds, woodlands and shoreline scrub. The **Lough Neagh Discovery Centre** here has audio-visual shows and interactive games, and visitors can participate in guided walks or take a boat trip.

For more seclusion, there are hides (camouflaged shelters) for birdwatching and a variety of marked walking trails.

✚ 9C

Lough Neagh Discovery Centre

✉ Oxford Island ☎ 028 3832 2205 🕓 Jul–Aug Mon–Fri 9–6, Sat–Sun 10–6; Sep–Jun Mon–Fri 9–5, Sat–Sun 10–6 ✋ Moderate 🍴 Cafe (££)

MOUNTAINS OF MOURNE

Percy French wrote many popular songs extolling the beauty of Ireland, but his best-known line must surely be *'where the Mountains of Mourne sweep down to the sea'*. Few first-time visitors, though, would be prepared for the wild beauty of the scenery.

The **Mourne Heritage Trust** at Newcastle is a good place to start, with lots of useful information and guided walks. One of the nature trails follows the 'Brandy Pad', a notorious smugglers' route that links Hilltown, notable for its many pubs, with the coast south of Newcastle.

Slieve Donard, at 839m (2,752ft), is the highest mountain, and clothing its slopes is the Donard Forest Park. There is more woodland in the Tollymore and Castlewellan forest parks, while to the south is the evocatively named Silent Valley, flooded to form two great reservoirs. There is a charge for cars to enter the forest parks and Silent Valley, which are accessible from about 10am (closing time varies depending on the season).

➕ 10D

Mourne Heritage Trust

www.mournelive.com

✉ 87 Central Promenade, Newcastle ☎ 028 4372 4059 🕐 Mon–Fri 9–5

🖐 Free

MOUNT STEWART HOUSE AND GARDENS

One of Ireland's grandest stately homes, Mount Stewart was built for the 3rd Marquess of Londonderry. Three architects were involved in the building – James Wyatt, in the 1780s, then George Dance and (probably) William Vitruvious Morrison in the early 19th century. The imposing interior largely reflects the impeccable taste of the 7th Marchioness, a leader of London society in the 1920s and 1930s. She was also responsible for the garden, which benefits from the mild climate between the Irish Sea and Strangford Lough.

🖽 11C ✉ 8km (5 miles) southeast of Newtownards ☎ 028 4278 8387
🕔 Grounds: May–Sep daily 10–8; Apr, Oct daily 10–6; Nov–Mar daily 10–4.
House: Jun–Aug daily 12–6; May, Sep Mon, Wed–Fri 1–6, Sat–Sun 12–6;
mid-Mar to Apr, Oct Sat–Sun and public hols 12–6 🖐 Moderate
🍴 Tea room (£) 🚌 Ulsterbus 9 and 10 from Belfast–Portaferry 🚉 Bangor

ULSTER-AMERICAN FOLK PARK

Best places to see, ➤ 54–55.

ULSTER FOLK AND TRANSPORT MUSEUM

All kinds of Ulster buildings have been painstakingly dismantled in their original locations, brought to this 25ha (62-acre) site and reconstructed in appropriate settings, including a small town of the 1900s, complete with shops, a school, churches, printer's workshops, a bank and terraced (row) houses. Rural exhibits include traditional Irish cottages, watermills and farmhouses, and farming is represented by rare breeds of animals, and fields which are cultivated using traditional methods.

The Transport Museum is comprehensive, covering all forms of transport from horse-drawn carts to the De Lorean car, and

includes the superb Irish Railway Collection and the X2 Flight Experience, an interactive exhibition. Perennially popular is the *Titanic* exhibition, about the 'unsinkable' liner which was built in Belfast's shipyards and foundered after hitting an iceberg on its maiden voyage.

As well as the permanent exhibitions, the museum has special events, which change from year to year.

www.uftm.org.uk

🕂 10C ✉ Bangor Road, Cultra, Holywood ☎ 028 9042 8428 ⏱ Mar–Jun Mon–Fri 10–5, Sat 10–6, Sun 11–6; Jul–Sep Mon–Sat 10–6, Sun 11–6; Oct–Feb Mon–Fri 10–4, Sat 10–5, Sun 11–5 💷 Moderate 🍴 Tea room (£) 🚌 B1, B2 from Belfast to Bangor 🚆 Cultra Halt

WELLBROOK BEETLING MILL

This water-powered, 18th-century linen hammer mill, set in a lovely wooded glen on the banks of the fast-flowing River Ballinderry, is a testament to the history of linen-making in Northern Ireland. For much of the 19th century the north of Ireland was the world's greatest producer of linen and you can see demonstrations of how the material was made.

Tours are conducted around the mill, costumed interpreters explain the process of manufacture and you can try your hand at scutching, hackling, weaving and beetling. Beetling is the final process in linen manufacture, when the cloth is repeatedly hammered to produce a sheen – the heavy wooden hammers used were known as beetles. The process could last for anything between two days and two weeks. The mill's seven water-powered beetling engines create a thunderous noise and it was not unusual for the beetlers to become completely or partially deaf working in a confined space for up to 15 hours a day.

🕂 8C ✉ Wellbrook Road, Corkhill (6.5km/4 miles west of Cookstown) ☎ 028 8674 8210 ⏱ Apr–Jun, Sep Sat–Sun 2–6; Jul–Aug Sat–Thu 2–6 💷 Moderate 🚌 Ulsterbus 90 from Cookstown; request stop at Kildress then 1km (half-mile) walk ❓ Shop; scenic walks

HOTELS

ARMAGH, CO ARMAGH
Hillview Lodge (£)
Family-run guest house with good facilities in a rural setting just
1.5km (1 mile) from the city. Golf driving range.
✉ 33 Newtownhamilton Road ☎ 028 3752 2000; www.hillviewlodge.com

BALLINTOY, CO ANTRIM
Whitepark House (££)
Country house on the coast road between the Causeway and the
rope bridge.
✉ 150 Whitepark Road ☎ 028 2073 1482; www.whiteparkhouse.com

BELFAST, CO ANTRIM
Ash-Rowan Town House (££)
Former home of Thomas Andrews, designer of the *Titanic*. The
quality furnishings are popular with guests here.
✉ 12 Windsor Avenue ☎ 028 9066 1758

Hastings Europa Hotel (£££)
The Europa is a truly international hotel with excellent facilities and
was the choice of President Clinton during his visits to Belfast in
1995 and 1998. It was once famed for being 'the most bombed
hotel' but can now be described as luxurious.
✉ Great Victoria Street ☎ 028 9027 1066; www.hastingshotel.com

Jury's Inn Belfast (£–££)
In the heart of the city, next to the Opera House, a short walk from
the main shopping area.
✉ Fisherwick Place, Great Victoria Street ☎ 028 9053 3500;
www.jurysinns.com

CARNLOUGH, CO ANTRIM
Londonderry Arms Hotel (££–£££)
Famous for its food and its history, this fine Georgian house was
once owned by Sir Winston Churchill.
✉ 20 Harbour Road ☎ 028 2888 5255; www.glensofantrim.com

COLERAINE, CO LONDONDERRY
Breezemount House (£–££)
Restored 19th-century house offering superior bed-and-breakfast facilities. Rooms have private bathroom, kitchen and satellite TV.
✉ 26 Castlerock Road ☎ 028 7034 4615; www.breezemount.co.uk
🕐 Closed 24–28 Dec

DONEGAL, CO DONEGAL
Central Hotel (££–£££)
Family-run town-centre hotel with views over Donegal Bay from the garden.
✉ The Diamond ☎ 074-972 1027; www.whites-hotelsireland.com

ENNISKILLEN, CO FERMANAGH
Arch House Tullyhona (£)
Welcoming guest house, good for families with young children.
✉ 59 Marble Arch Road ☎ 028 6634 8452; www.archhouse.com

LONDONDERRY, CO LONDONDERRY
The Merchant's House (£)
This Victorian merchant's family home has been converted into one of the city's finest bed-and-breakfasts.
✉ 16 Queen Street ☎ 028 126423; www.thesaddlershouse.com

RESTAURANTS

ANNALONG, CO DOWN
Glassdrumman Lodge (£££)
Prime local produce, including prawns and salmon, feature on the six-course dinner menu of well-produced dishes.
✉ 85 Mill Road ☎ 028 4376 8451 🕐 Dinner; bookings essential

BALLYCASTLE, CO ANTRIM
Wysner's (£–££)
Pleasant two-storey restaurant in the centre of town, with reasonably priced dishes, including traditional Irish and a good selection of healthy eating options.
✉ 16 Ann Street ☎ 028 2076 2372 🕐 Lunch, dinner; closed Sun

BALLYMENA, CO ANTRIM
Galgorm Resort and Spa (£££)
The restaurant of this restored 19th-century mansion offers fine dining overlooking the River Maine.
✉ 136 Fenaghy Road ☎ 028 2588 1001 🕐 Lunch, dinner

BANGOR, CO DOWN
Clandeboye Lodge Hotel (£–££)
Interesting treatment of good local produce in a secluded location.
✉ 10 Estate Road, Clandeboye ☎ 028 9185 2500 🕐 Lunch, dinner, bar food; closed 24–26 Dec

BELFAST, CO ANTRIM
Morning Star (££)
An historic Belfast pub with exceptionally good food, using only the freshest Ulster produce and seafood.
✉ 17 Pottinger's Entry ☎ 028 9032 5986 🕐 Lunch daily, dinner Mon–Sat

Nick's Warehouse (£–££)
See page 59.

The Northern Wing (£–££)
Caesar salad, beef and Guinness sausages, salmon goujons (strips) and more served in this old printing press now restored into a stylish restaurant.
✉ 2 Bridge Street ☎ 028 9050 9888 🕐 All day menu

DONEGAL, CO DONEGAL
Harbour Restaurant (£–££)
Cosy restaurant with a good variety of international and Irish dishes.
✉ Quay Street ☎ 074-972 1702 🕐 Lunch Sun, dinner daily

ENNISKILLEN, CO FERMANAGH
Killyhevlin Hotel (£–££)
Excellent food and wonderful views over Lough Erne.
✉ Dublin Road, Killyhevlin ☎ 028 6632 3481 🕐 Breakfast, lunch, dinner

HILLSBOROUGH, CO DOWN
Hillside Restaurant and Bar (££)
Traditional country-house cooking with global influences.
✉ 21 Main Street ☎ 028 9268 2765 🕐 Bar: lunch, dinner. Restaurant: dinner Fri, Sat; closed evenings Good Fri and 25 Dec

KILLYLEAGH, CO DOWN
Dufferin Arms (£–££)
European, seafood and vegetarian choices feature heavily on the menu at this well-known country pub.
✉ 35 High Street ☎ 028 4482 1182 🕐 Lunch, dinner

LIMAVADY, CO LONDONDERRY
The Lime Tree (££)
Modern Irish cuisine using the best of seasonal local produce.
✉ 60 Catherine Street ☎ 028 7776 4300 🕐 Dinner only Tue–Sat; closed 25–26 Dec

LONDONDERRY, CO LONDONDERRY
Beech Hill Country House Hotel (££–£££)
This exclusive hotel, in a peaceful location in 13ha (32 acres) of glorious woodlands, has an excellent restaurant.
✉ 32 Ardmore Road ☎ 028 7134 9279; www.beech-hill.com 🕐 Breakfast, lunch, dinner; closed 25 Dec

OMAGH, CO TYRONE
Mellon Country Inn (££)
The Mellon serves up traditional Irish cuisine with a modern twist.
✉ 134 Beltany Road ☎ 028 8166 1224 🕐 Lunch, dinner

PORTAFERRY, CO DOWN
Portaferry Hotel (£££)
A charming 18th-century inn picturesquely set on the edge of Strangford Lough. The restaurant is best known for its seafood.
✉ 10 The Strand ☎ 028 4272 8231 🕐 Lunch, early evening menu, à la carte dinner; closed 24–25 Dec

SHOPPING

CRAFTS

Bonners of Ardara

Bonners, world-renowned for the quality of its knitwear, has a factory in the town and employs more than 500 hand-knitters throughout Donegal. Also sells Waterford Crystal, Belleek and Donegal china, jewellery, linens and tweeds.

✉ Front Street, Ardara, Co Donegal ☎ 074-954 1303 🕓 May–Jun Mon–Sat 9–6:30; Jul–Aug Mon–Sat 10–7, Sun 10–6; Sep–Apr Mon–Tue Thu–Sat 10–6

Conway Mill Craft Shop

Over 22 artists work and display their work in the craft shop, which sometimes hosts other events such as book or poetry readings. Items of contemporary and Irish art. Also guided tours of the mill.

✉ 5–7 Conway Street, Belfast, Co Antrim ☎ 028 9032 6452
🕓 Mon–Fri 10–4

Derry Craft Village

Craftspeople ply their trade in an 18th-century setting.

✉ Shipquay Street, Londonderry, Co Londonderry ☎ 028 7126 0329
🕓 Daily 9–6 or 7

Donegal Craft Village

Variety of items, including pottery, Uilleann pipes, jewellery, batik and woven goods. Coffee shop.

✉ Ballyshannon Road, Donegal, Co Donegal ☎ 074-972 2225 🕓 Mon–Sat 10–5:30 (sometimes closed winter)

Tyrone Crystal

Guided tour takes in all the stages of producing fine crystal, from glass-blowing to cutting and finishing.

✉ Killybrackey, Coalisland Road, Dungannon, Co Tyrone ☎ 028 8772 5335
🕓 Shop: Mon–Sat 9:30–5, Sun 1–5 (seasonal). Tours: Mon–Fri 11, 12, 2

The Wicker Man

Highly regarded craft shop showcasing work by over 150 Irish craftspeople.

✉ 14 Donegal Arcade, Castle Place, Belfast, Co Antrim ☎ 028 8772 5335
🕒 Mon–Sat 9–5

DEPARTMENT STORE
Magee's
A legend in the world of department stores, run by the same family since 1866. The speciality is hand-woven Donegal tweed; guided tours of original looms at work.
✉ The Diamond, Donegal, Co Donegal ☎ 074-9722660 🕒 Mon–Sat 9:30–6

MARKET
St George's Market
Built in 1896, the market has had a face-lift.
✉ Oxford Street/May Street, Belfast, Co Antrim 🕒 Fri morning and Sat 10–4

TRADITIONAL MUSIC
Premier Record Store
Specializes in traditional CDs and tapes. Behind Castle Court Shopping Centre.
✉ 3–5 Smithfield Square North, Belfast, Co Antrim ☎ 028 9024 0896
🕒 Mon–Sat 9–5:30

ENTERTAINMENT

LIVE MUSIC
Dungloe Bar
✉ Waterloo Street, Londonderry, Co Londonderry ☎ 028 7126 7716

John Hewitt Bar
In the heart of the Cathedral quarter, this very traditional bar stages jazz on Friday and traditional music on Tuesday, Wednesday and Saturday.
✉ 51 Donegall Street, Belfast, Co Antrim ☎ 028 9023 3768

Robinsons
Five bars, each with it's own style.
✉ 38–42 Great Victoria Street, Belfast, Co Antrim ☎ 028 9024 7447

Rotterdam Bar
Probably the most famous of Belfast's music pubs.
✉ 54 Pilot Street, Belfast, Co Antrim ☎ 028 9074 6021

NIGHTCLUBS
Club Milk
Offers a varied spectrum of music, from house to disco.
✉ 10–14 Tomb Street, Belfast, Co Antrim ☎ 028 9027 8876 🕙 Nightly

The Fly Bar
Sophisticated cocktails and Cool FM DJs.
✉ 5–6 Lower Crescent, Belfast, Co Antrim ☎ 028 9050 9750

Front Page
Pub club with live bands.
✉ Lower Donegall Street, Belfast, Co Antrim ☎ 028 9032 4924

THEATRE AND CINEMA
The Movie House
On Tuesdays you can watch any film for just £2.50.
✉ York Street, Belfast, Co Antrim ☎ 028 9075 5000

Nerve Centre
Innovative, multimedia arts centre.
✉ 7–8 Magazine Street, Londonderry, Co Londonderry ☎ 028 7126 0562

Old Museum Arts Centre
A venue for experimental theatre, dance, storytelling and poetry.
✉ College Square North, Belfast, Co Antrim ☎ 028 9023 3332

Queen's Film Theatre
Shows the best in new and classic world cinema.
✉ University Square Mews, Belfast, Co Antrim ☎ 0800 9097 1097

Verbal Arts Centre
Children's events, storytelling and more.
✉ London Street, Londonderry, Co Londonderry ☎ 028 7126 6946

Sight Locator Index

This index relates to the maps on the covers. We have given map references to the main sights of interest in the book. Grid references in italics indicate sights featured on the town plans. Some sights within towns may not be plotted on the maps.

Index

Acknowledgements

The Automobile Association would like to thank the following photographers and companies for their assistance in the preparation of this book.

Abbreviations for the picture credits are as follows – (t) top; (b) bottom; (c) centre; (l) left; (r) right; (AA) AA World Travel Library

4l Dunmanus Bay, Co Cork, AA/J Blandford; **4c** Ferries at Rosslare, AA/C Jones; **4r** St Candice Cathedral, Kilkenny, AA/M Short; **5l** Ha'Penny Bridge, over River Liffey, Dublin, © Ingolf Pompe 64/Alamy; **5c** Powerscourt Estate, AA/L Blake; **6/7** Dunmanus Bay, Co Cork, AA/J Blandford; **8/9** St Colman's Cathedral, Cobh, AA/O Forss; **10/11t** O'Connell Street, Dublin, AA/S Day; **10cl** Rock of Cashel, AA/S McBride; **10cr** Dingle, AA/C Jones; **11c** Bar, Dublin, AA/S Whitehorne; **11b** Pony trap, Muckross estate, AA/J Blandford; **12b** Powerscourt Shopping Centre, Dublin, AA/M Short; **13tr** English Market, Cork, AA/S Hill; **13c** Food market, Dublin, AA/S Day; **14l** St Patrick's Street, Cork, AA/C Jones; **14r** Old Jameson Distillery, Dublin, AA/S Day; **15t** Guinness, AA/C Coe; **15b** Dublin, AA/S McBride; **16/17t** Grafton Street, Dublin, AA/S Day; **16/17c** The Curragh, AA/C Coe; **16b** Derrynane and the Ring of Kerry, AA/J Blandford; **17b** Cliffs of Moher, AA/P Zollier; **18** Giant's Causeway, AA/C Hill; **19t** Galway Oyster Festival, AA/S McBride; **19b** Athlone Castle, AA/L Blake; **20/21** Ferries at Rosslare, AA/C Jones; **25** Galway oyster festival, AA/S McBride; **27** Lough Leane, Co Kerry, AA/J Blandford; **28** Road between Glengarriff and Kenmare, AA; **29** Road signs, AA/M Diggin; **32/33** Garda car, AA/J Dawson; **34/35** St Candice Cathedral, Kilkenny, AA/M Short; **36/37t** Inscribed stones, AA/M Short; **36/37b** Newgrange, AA/P Zollier; **37cl** Mace head, Knowth, AA/C Coe; **38bl** Nun's Church, AA/C Coe; **38/39** Clonmacnois, AA/L Blake; **39tr** Bay near Clonmacnois, AA/S McBride; **40t** Dingle, AA/C Jones; **40c** Stone cross, Kilmalkedar Church, AA/C Jones; **41** Slea head, Dingle peninsula, AA/C Jones; **42/43** Giant's Causeway, AA/C Coe; **44cl** Kilkenny, AA/S McBride; **44bl** Kilkenny, AA/S McBride; **45** Kilkenny Castle, AA/C Jones; **46** Muckross House, AA/J Blandford; **46/47b** Muckross House, K Welsh/Alamy; **48/49t** National Museum, AA/S Whitehorne; **48b** National Museum, AA/S Day; **50t** Celtic cross, Inishmore, AA/S Hill; **50c** Dun Aengus, Inishmore Island, AA/S Hill; **51** Collecting seaweed, AA/Stephen Hill; **52** Rock of Cashel, AA/S McBride; **53tl** Shamrock motif, Rock of Cashel, AA/S McBride; **53tr** Tomb, Rock of Cashel, AA/S McBride; **54/55t** 19th-century street of shops, Ulster-American Folk Park; **54c** Mellon farmhouse, Ulster-American Folk Park; **56/57** Ha'Penny Bridge, over River Liffey, Dublin, © Ingolf Pompe 64/Alamy; **58** Restaurant, Dublin, AA/S McBride; **61** Dublin Castle, Record Tower, AA/S Day; **62/63** Connemara National Park, AA/C Jones; **65** Golfers, Ballybunion, AA/P Zollier; **66/67** Lough Erne, Co Kerry, AA/C Coe; **68** Belleek Pottery workshop, AA/J Johnson; **70/71bg** Viking Splash Tour, AA/S Day; **73** Fitzsimon's Inn, Dublin, AA/S Day; **74** Christ Church Cathedral, AA/S Whitehorne; **75tl** Dublin Castle, AA/S Day; **75tr** Temple Bar, AA/S Day; **76** Monument to W B Yeats, Sligo Town, AA/C Hill; **77** Shaw Birthplace, Dublin, AA/S Day; **78/79** Powerscourt Estate, AA/L Blake; **81** South cross, Kells, AA/P Zollier; **83t** Record Tower, Dublin Castle, AA/S Day; **83b** Brendan Behan's typewriter, AA/S Day; **84** Atrium, Guinness Storehouse; **85t** Guinness Storehouse; **85b** Kilmainham Gaol AA/S Whitehorne; **86** National Gallery, AA/Slide File; **87** Old Jameson Distillery, AA/S Day; **88l** Trinity College, AA/L Blake; **88/89** Temple Bar, AA/S Whitehorne; **90/91** Castletown House, AA/M Short; **92t** Glendalough, AA/C Jones; **92cb** Glendalough, AA/C Jones; **93b** Irish National Heritage Park, AA/P Zollier; **94l** Jerpoint Abbey, AA/M Short; **95t** Japanese Gardens, AA/S McBride; **95c** Japanese Gardens, AA/M Short; **96/97** Malahide Castle, AA/Slide File; **97r** Cross of Muiredach, AA/C Jones; **98tr** Powerscourt Gardens, AA/M Short; **99** Wexford AA/S Day; **100/101** Powerscourt, AA/M Short; **102** Lough Tay, Wicklow Mountains, AA/C Jones; **111** Cork, AA/S McBride; **112** St Finbarr's Cathedral and South Gate Bridge, AA/C Jones; **113r** Tribute to Rory Gallagher, AA/C Jones; **115** St Anne's Church, K Welsh/Alamy; **116** Bridge in Cork, AA/J Blandford; **117** St Patrick's Street, AA/J Blandford; **118t** Bantry Bay, AA/M Diggin; **118b** Garinish Island, AA/J Blandford; **119** Blarney Castle, AA/S McBride; **120/121** Rock of Cashel, AA/S McBride; **122l** Ring of Kerry, AA/J Blandford; **122/123** Jaunting car, Gap of Dunloe, AA/S McBride; **123r** Killarney, AA/J Blandford; **124/125** Killarney National Park, AA/S McBride; **126t** Kinsale, AA/O Forss; **126c** Kinsale, AA/S McBride; **127** Limerick, AA/P Zollier; **128** Christ Church Cathedral Precinct, AA/M Short; **137** The Burren, AA/S McBride; **138** Cathedral of St Nicholas and Our Lady Assumed into Heaven, AA/C Hill; **140** Galway City, © Vincent MacNamara/Alamy; **141** Statue of Padraic O Conaire, Eyre Square, AA/S McBride; **142** Bunratty Castle, AA/P Zollier; **143** The Burren, AA/S McBride; **144/145** Connemara National Park, AA/C Hill; **145br** Aughanure Castle, AA/C Jones; **146bl** Roundstone harbour, AA/L Blake; **147** Clifden, AA/L Blake; **148/149** Kylemore Abbey, AA/L Blake; **149br** King John's Castle, Athlone, AA/L Blake; **150t** Sligo, AA/J Dawson; **150/151b** Westport House, AA/L Blake; **151r** Thoor Ballylee, AA/S McBride; **159** Royal Opera House, Belfast, AA/I Dawson; **160** Crown Liquor Saloon, Belfast, AA/C Coe; **161** Palm House, Botanic Gardens, AA/G Munday; **162t** City Hall, AA/I Dawson; **162b** Crown Liquor Saloon, AA/G Munday; **163** Queen's University, Belfast, © J Orr/Alamy; **164** Ulster Museum, AA; **165t** Grand Opera House, AA/G Munday; **166** Palace stables, Armagh, AA/I Dawson; **167b** Fair Head from Ballycastle Bay, AA/M Diggin; **168** Carrickfergus Castle, AA/D Forss; **169** Pottery wheel at Donegal Craft Village, AA/C Hill; **171** Dunluce Castle, AA/C Coe; **172t** Waterfall in Glenariff, AA/C Coe; **173c** Peace statue, Londonderry, AA/C Coe; **174/175** Carrick-a-Rede Rope Bridge, AA/G Munday; **176** Lough Neagh, AA/G Munday; **177** Tollymore Forest Park, AA; **178** Mount Stewart, AA/G Munday.

Every effort has been made to trace the copyright holders, and we apologise in advance for any accidental errors. We would be happy to apply the corrections in the following edition of this publication.

Dear Reader

Your comments, opinions and recommendations are very important to us. Please help us to improve our travel guides by taking a few minutes to complete this simple questionnaire.

You do not need a stamp (unless posted outside the UK). If you do not want to cut this page from your guide, then photocopy it or write your answers on a plain sheet of paper.

Send to: **The Editor, AA World Travel Guides,
FREEPOST SCE 4598, Basingstoke RG21 4GY.**

Your recommendations...

We always encourage readers' recommendations for restaurants, nightlife or shopping – if your recommendation is used in the next edition of the guide, we will send you a **FREE AA Guide** of your choice from this series. Please state below the establishment name, location and your reasons for recommending it.

_____
_____
_____
_____
_____
_____

Please send me **AA Guide** _____

About this guide...

Which title did you buy?

AA _____

Where did you buy it?_____

When? m m / y y

Why did you choose this guide? _____

_____
_____
_____
_____

Did this guide meet your expectations?

Exceeded ☐   Met all ☐   Met most ☐   Fell below ☐

Were there any aspects of this guide that you particularly liked? _____

_____
_____
_____

continued on next page...

Is there anything we could have done better? _____

_____

_____

_____

About you...

Name (*Mr/Mrs/Ms*) _____

Address _____

_____

_____ Postcode _____

Daytime tel nos _____

Email _____

Please only give us your mobile phone number or email if you wish to hear from us about other products and services from the AA and partners by text or mms, or email.

Which age group are you in?
Under 25 ☐   25–34 ☐   35–44 ☐   45–54 ☐   55–64 ☐   65+ ☐

How many trips do you make a year?
Less than one ☐   One ☐   Two ☐   Three or more ☐

Are you an AA member? Yes ☐   No ☐

About your trip...

When did you book? m m / y y   When did you travel? m m / y y

How long did you stay? _____

Was it for business or leisure? _____

Did you buy any other travel guides for your trip? _____

If yes, which ones? _____

_____

_____

Thank you for taking the time to complete this questionnaire. Please send it to us as soon as possible, and remember, you do not need a stamp (*unless posted outside the UK*).

AA Travel Insurance call 0800 072 4168 or visit www.theAA.com